The Sophisticated... OLIVE

THE COMPLETE GUIDE TO OLIVE CUISINE

MARIE NADINE ANTOL

SQUAREONE
PUBLISHERS

Cover Designer: Phaedra Mastrocola • Cover Photo: Rob Melnychuk/Getty Images
Text Illustrator: Kathe Cobb • Typesetter: Gary A. Rosenberg • Editor: Joanne Abrams

Square One Publishers • 115 Herricks Road • Garden City Park, NY 11040 • (516) 535-2010
www.squareonepublishers.com

Permission Credits
    The photos on pages 4, 11, 20, 24, 36, 37, and 92 were reprinted courtesy of
    Kotinos Organic Olive Oil.

    The photos on pages 15, 16, and 26 were reprinted courtesy of the Lewis
    Baer collection, Penngrove, California.

    The photo on page 14 was reprinted courtesy of FreeStock Photos.com.

    The photo on page 48 was reprinted courtesy of Olive Pit at olivepit.com.

Library of Congress Cataloging-in-Publication Data

Antol, Marie Nadine.
  The sophisticated olive : the complete guide to olive cuisine / Marie
Nadine Antol.
    p. cm.
Includes index.
  ISBN 0-7570-0024-X (pbk.)
  1. Cookery (Olives) 2. Cookery (Olive oil) 3. Olive. I. Title.
TX813.O4 A54 2004
641.3'463—dc21
                                    2002010513

Printed in the United States of America

10   9   8   7   6   5   4   3   2   1

Contents

Preface, v

Introduction, 1

PART ONE

The **Life** and **Times** of the **Olive**

1. The History of the Olive, 7
2. From Tree to Table, 19
3. Olives of the World, 31
4. Olives, Health, and Beauty, 49
5. Olives in Your Own Backyard, 75

PART TWO

The **Tastes** and **Pleasures** of the **Olive**

6. The Art of Olive Making, 95
7. Cooking With Olives and Olive Oil, 111
   Conclusion, 183

Metric Conversion Tables, 184
Resource List, 185
Index, 187

Preface

I have been enamored of the sophisticated olive for a very long time. Growing up, there were always several jars of olives in the refrigerator—shiny black olives with mellow flesh, as well as big green Spanish olives stuffed with pimento. Looking back, I realize now that that it wasn't a very big selection. Nonetheless, I can trace my insatiable appetite for olives to that time. We always had a dish of olives and celery in the dining room, which was common in those days. I skipped the celery, but savored every bite of the olives.

Given my fondness for this delicious fruit, as you may imagine, this book has been a delight to both research and write. I have met some very special people along the way. And whether they were growers, canners, or involved in trade associations, both national and international, all were generous in sharing their expertise, some in personal conversations and others via e-mail or "snail" mail. Unfortunately, it is impossible to mention the names of all of the people who enriched this book by providing helpful information. However, in three cases, I would be truly remiss if I did not include my grateful acknowledgments.

First, I'd like to thank Peter Hatch, Director of Gardens and Grounds at Monticello. Warm, friendly, and funny, he brought me up-to-date on Thomas Jefferson's efforts to grow olives in his garden. You'll find this story in Chapter 5, "Olives in Your Own Backyard."

Second, I wish to thank Jennifer Davis of Big Trees Now/Pleasure Point Landscape. Jennifer generously provided specific information that will guide you in growing your very own olive tree and harvesting your own crop of olives. (Again, see Chapter 5.)

Finally, I thank the people at the University of California, Division of Agricultural Sciences, for their instruction in the various methods of curing olives at home. You'll learn how to do this yourself in Part Two, "The Tastes and Pleasures of the Olive."

I truly enjoyed experimenting with the many recipes that you'll find in Chapter 7, "Cooking With Olives and Olive Oil." These recipes came from many sources; some were based on dishes in very old cookbooks, some came from family and friends, and some I devised on my own. I don't think I've ever made anything the same way twice, so settling on a final version wasn't easy for me, but in each case, I persevered until I was satisfied with the results. I promise you that everything is delicious, so browse a bit and make something wonderful for your family. Don't fail to try the olive breads. They may be my crowning achievements.

In short, I had a very good time writing this book. My family and friends enjoyed taste-testing my creations—some new and adventurous, some familiar and down-home. I know that your family and friends will also revel in the delights of olive cuisine, and that these dishes will enhance your appreciation of the sophisticated olive.

Introduction

Since you are holding this book in your hand, chances are that you're a lover of olives. If so, congratulations! You are exhibiting superb taste. Like the appreciation of fine wine, the love of olives is a sophisticated one that is cultivated over time. This book is going to introduce you to the finest olives in the world, and perhaps refine your palate even further. And if you are not yet an olive aficionado, perhaps these pages will be the beginning of a new culinary adventure—an adventure that will enhance the foods you already enjoy, and add an array of wonderful new delicacies to your life.

The Sophisticated Olive has been designed as a tour of the world of olives. There's so much to learn about the olive in all its guises—not just the fruit and the oil, but also the leaves and the bark. The olive itself is both food and medicine; the leaves and the bark are natural medicinals; and the expressed oil is used for preserving foods and cooking gastronomical delights. You're going to discover many secrets in this book—secrets that will amaze you, delight you, and even amuse you.

Part One, "The Life and Times of the Olive," opens with a fascinating look at the history of the olive. According to various myths, olives were a gift from the gods, but different cultures give the credit to different deities. After exploring the most famous of these legends, Chapter 1 walks you through the olive's historical beginnings, starting with mankind's earliest experiences with this amazing fruit and ending with the tree's introduction to the New World. The olive has had many adventures on its travels from the shores of the Mediterranean to your table today. I think you'll enjoy the journey.

Chapter 2 is where you'll learn all about *Olea europaea*, the extraordinary plant that is the subject of this book. Here, you'll find out how the olive tree grows, and you'll discover how its wonderful fruit is harvested and either made into tantalizing table olives or turned into golden olive oil. Included in this chapter is a clear explanation of the various forms of olive oil, from pure extra virgin oil to specialty oils that have been infused with the flavor and aroma of fresh herbs.

Chapter 3 will take you on a country-by-country tour of the world of olives. What makes the flavor and color of Greece's Kalamata olives so special? Which country's "ripe" olives are not really ripe at all? Chapter 3 tells all, and also includes a handy guide to the most delectable olives available.

For many people, Chapter 4, "Olives, Health, and Beauty," will be the most eye-opening chapter of all. You probably already know that in addition to boasting a wonderfully fruity taste, olive oil is thought to be the most heart-healthy fat on the planet. But perhaps you're not aware that this lovely oil is also a remarkable cosmetic that has been relied on by legendary beauties for centuries. Even the olive leaf has been found to have extraordinary properties.

Chapter 5 is an introduction to growing an olive tree in your own backyard. Is it possible to produce your own olives even if you live in the northern climes of the United States rather than the shores of the Mediterranean? The answer is "yes"—provided that your tree is container-grown and brought indoors during harsh winter weather. This chapter will guide you through the process, from the selection and planting of the tree to the first miraculous harvest.

Whether you grow your own olive tree or, like most of us, you buy both your olives and your oil in a store, you'll want to spend some time browsing through Part Two, "The Tastes and Pleasures of the Olive." First, Chapter 6 will introduce you to the art of olive making. Just as you can grow your own olives, you can home-cure them, too. In this chapter, you'll learn how to make several different types, from Spanish-Style Green Olives to Hot and Spicy Sicilian-Style Olives.

Once your olives have been cured—or you've simply stocked your pantry with high-quality olives and olive oil—you're ready to start cooking. In Chapter 7, you'll find a tantalizing collection of recipes from around the world that rely on the olive and olive oil for luscious flavor. If you always wanted to make the perfect martini (or dirty martini), you'll find out just how it's done. This chapter also offers recipes for everything from marinades to salad dressings, from unusual salads to entrées. You'll even find some olive-kissed desserts. (Really!) Every recipe is hand-selected, kitchen-tested, and guaranteed to please.

As I said earlier, the love of olives is one that's acquired over time. I hope that this book will help you further cultivate your appreciation of this miraculous fruit, and guide you in enhancing each and every day with the charms of the sophisticated olive.

PART ONE

The Life & Times of the Olive

CHAPTER 1

The **History** of the **Olive**

For the Lord thy God bringeth thee into a good land,
a land of brooks of water, of fountains and depths
that spring out of valleys and hills; A land of wheat,
and barley and vines, and fig trees, and pomegranates;
a land of oil olive, and honey . . .

—DEUTERONOMY 8:7–8

The history of the olive is as old as the history of civilization. In fact, the domestication of olives actually predates recorded history. For thousands of years, olives—and the "liquid gold" called olive oil—were not just food, but also medicine and magic to people throughout the Mediterranean. Later, the olive spread from the Old World to the New, where it helped fuel the growth of the United States. This is what makes the history of the olive so fascinating. It takes you on a journey from the groves of Greece to the valleys of California. It involves all aspects of life, from medicine to the military. And it is at the heart of many religions, from the mythology of the ancient Greeks to the beliefs of the Jews, Christians, and Muslims.

LEGENDS AND MYTHS

Some authorities claim that the olive was born in the Garden of Eden. Not so, say the Egyptians. They insist that the olive was a magnificent gift from the goddess Isis. Oh, no, say the Greeks. It wasn't Isis who brought the olive to mankind. The first olive tree was a gift to man from the Greek goddess Athena. Let's look at this last legend—the most famous one about the birth of the olive.

According to Greek mythology, both Athena and Poseidon once loved a beautiful city in Greece and wanted it for their own. Zeus declared that the people of the city would worship whichever god provided them with the most useful gift. Poseidon struck a rock with his trident and brought forth either salt or a horse, depending on the account. Athena, however, conjured up a full-grown olive tree bursting with fruit. Zeus plucked a ripe fruit, bit into it, and was pleased beyond measure by its richness and flavor. On the spot, he decreed that the olive tree was the most valuable gift mankind would ever receive. I'd like to have one of Athena's trees myself. Fresh olives are very bitter. If Zeus enjoyed an olive of incomparable flavor straight off the tree, it appears that Athena's tree bore olives that were magically cured on the branch. At any rate, in return for the gift of the olive tree, the Greeks named the city of Athens after her. Greek coins bearing the image of Athena picture the goddess holding a two-handled vessel containing olive oil, with an olive wreath crowning her helmet.

There are other Greek legends, as well. One story is that Hercules, the hero of extraordinary strength, planted his favorite walking staff in the fertile ground of Greece, where it promptly sprouted leaves and miraculously

According to Greek mythology, the olive tree was a gift to mankind from the goddess Athena. In return for this wondrous plant, the Greeks named the city of Athens after her.

Rich Olive Traditions

Laurel leaves were once used to crown heroes, and mistletoe is forever linked with kissing. But perhaps no plant is at the center of more traditions than the olive tree. Cultures have done far more than enjoy the olive and its wonderful oil. They have used this ancient plant as a symbol, an emblem, a tribute. Here are just some of the ways in which the olive has been made part of rich traditions.

❏ In ancient times, Chinese elders made apology to an offended clan by sending ahead an olive wrapped in red paper. When such a gift was received, the sender was assured that the quarrel would be forgotten and peace would be restored between the families. In fact, many cultures have viewed the olive as a symbol of peace. Eirene, the Greek goddess of peace, was depicted carrying an olive branch. And in modern times, the olive branch was incorporated into the seal of the United Nations.

❏ Ebla, an ancient Middle Eastern city-state located near the site of present-day Aleppo, Syria, offered the oil of the olive to their gods in tribute.

❏ The torch at the first Olympic Games was the burning branch of an olive tree. And olive oil, believed to confer strength and youth, was rubbed over the bodies of ancient Greek athletes.

❏ The caesars of Rome wore gold olive leaf crowns—symbols of benediction and purification.

❏ The original Festival of Chanukah, which celebrated the victory of the Maccabees and the re-dedication of the Temple at Jerusalem, was marked by the burning of so much olive oil that, we are told, the night was as bright as the day. Now, during the Feast of Lights, many Jews light olive oil-burning menorahs in memory of the oil that was used in the Temple at the time of its rededication.

grew into an olive tree bearing ripe fruit. And Pindar, the Greek lyric poet of the fifth century BCE, recounts how Hercules brought "the silver olive tree" home to Greece to make it a symbol of the Olympic Games.

However the olive tree came into being, it quickly assumed an important role in every early civilization. Let's continue the story.

THE WORLDWIDE TRAVELS OF THE OLIVE

Mythology aside, experts say that wild olives have thrived in the Mediterranean region for many thousands of years. Fossilized remains of olive leaves, discovered on the island of Santorini in the Aegean sea, have been carbon-dated to 37,000 BCE.

The exact origin of the olive tree has been lost in time, mingling with the development of the Mediterranean civilizations that left their mark on Western culture. Many experts believe that the wild olive tree was first born and cultivated in Phoenicia, an ancient maritime country that was located in present-day Syria and Lebanon, and that from there, the plant was spread by the Phoenicians to the Greeks. Others claim that cultivation began in Palestine. And still others maintain that cultivation began in Greece itself. We do know that in 3500 BCE, the edible olive was grown in Crete, and that until 1500 BCE, Greece was the most cultivated area. So we will continue our story of the olive with a visit to Greece.

The Olive Takes Root in Greece

By Homeric times, olives had become a staple food of the Greeks. Early Greek literature is rich with references to the fruit of the olive tree, and Homer himself referred to the oil of the olive as "liquid gold."

Earlier in the chapter, you learned that the ancient Greeks believed olives to be a gift of the gods. The importance of the olive to ancient Greece was further highlighted by the epic poet Homer (c. 850 BCE), who called olive oil "liquid gold." And the tree gained even greater importance a few centuries later when Solon (c. 639–559 BCE), the Athenian lawgiver and poet, issued decrees that regulated olive planting. Because the olive tree was considered sacred and was a national symbol of peace and wisdom, anyone who willfully uprooted or destroyed one was hauled into court. If found guilty, the punishment was death or exile. The olive was so revered in ancient Greece that only virgins and unbearded young men sworn to a life of chastity were considered pure enough to harvest the fruit.

You probably know that the Olympic Games originated in Greece. What you may not know is that the olive tree was the symbol of the Olympic contests. The first Olympic Games were held in 776 BCE, and it is believed that the original Olympic torch was a flaming olive branch. In addition, warm olive oil was rubbed over the skin of athletes, not only because it helped keep their muscles supple, but also because the olive was believed to impart strength. Athletes or not, both Greek and Roman aristocrats also enjoyed the oily ministrations of masseurs. The *strigil*, an instrument shaped like a small scythe, was invented by the Greeks to scrape away excess oil from the body.

The appearance of olive motifs in ancient artwork testifies to the fruit's importance in early civilizations. Ancient pottery, coins, and other objects were often adorned with images of olive trees, olive harvests, or vessels of olive oil.

As time went on, the olive played a critical role in every aspect of Greek life. Pedanius Dioscorides, a Greek physician and pharmacologist of the first century CE, wrote at length of the healthful benefits and curative properties of the olive and its oil. And in the second century, Athenaeus, a Greek citizen who was born in Egypt, wrote the fifteen-volume *Deipnosophistai* (The Gastronomers), which discusses the use of olive oil in the baking of bread, and the inclusion of olives in the meals of rich and poor alike. Olive oil was also infused with grasses and flowers and used as a cosmetic. And ships were built for the sole purpose of transporting olive oil to trading posts around the Mediterranean.

If you are not yet convinced of the significant role played by the olive in Greece, consider that in ancient times, it has been estimated that every citizen made use of nearly 20 gallons of olive oil annually—5.2 gallons in the diet, 7.8 gallons for personal hygiene, 3.2 quarts for lighting, 2.1 quarts for use in rituals, and 1.1 pints for medicine.

Of course, olives continue to figure largely in Greek life. To this day, olive trees dominate the rocky countryside, and people come from all over Greece and Europe to pick the fruit of the trees at harvest time. You'll learn more about the olives of Greece in Chapter 3.

The Olive Arrives in Italy

As olives gained importance in their diet, ancient Romans advanced the art of curing and seasoning the marvelous fruit. For instance, the Romans were the first to use wood ash and slaked lime to leach out the olive's bitterness.

Sometime around the sixth century BCE, Greek traders brought olive oil and young trees first to the island of Sicily, and then to southern Italy. Cultivation moved upwards, from the south of Italy to the north.

Very quickly, the olives of Italy became as interwoven with the fabric of everyday life as they had in Greece. Even aristocratic Romans, who had the gold to buy whatever they wanted, typically breakfasted on olives and bread. Conquering legions were honored with olives, and Roman caesars were crowned with wreaths of gold olive leaves and anointed with olive oil. Gladiators were, too. In fact, it is said that the sweaty olive oil sluiced from the bodies of famous gladiators was carefully collected in bowls bearing the gladiator's name. This sweat, full of the odoriferous pheromones we now know are sexual triggers, was considered highly desirable. Roman matrons paid exorbitant sums for a bowlful, and cosmetic formulators included the coveted product in some of their most costly lotions and potions.

Surviving writings testify to the importance of the olive tree in ancient Rome. In his work on farming, Cato the Elder (234–149 BCE), a Roman statesman, wrote extensively on the olive, detailing instructions for laying out a grove, planting the trees, pruning the branches, and expressing the oil. For a grove of 60 hectares (150 acres), Cato specified the need for three large carts, six plows and plowshares, three yokes, one harrow, manure hampers and baskets, three pack saddles, and three pads for the asses. According to Cato, the workers required to tend the olives included an overseer, three teamsters, a muleteer, and five laborers. It was mandated that the family holdings be equipped with oil presses and containers for the expressed oil. Cato even gave hundreds of uses for the watery black liquid that is left under the oil after olives have been pressed. Today, that liquid is discarded.

In one of the thirty-seven volumes of his encyclopedic *Natural History*, Pliny the Elder (23–79 CE), Roman scholar and naturalist, also had much to say about the olive. According to Pliny, the Romans preferred their olive oil green and freshly pressed. He conveyed the universal opinion of the day when he wrote, "The riper the berry, the more greasy and less pleasant is the flavor of the oil. The best time for gathering olives, striking a balance between quality and quantity, is when the berries just begin to turn dark." Pliny went on to assure his readers that "Italy has excellent olive oil at reasonable prices."

Olives and olive oil were among the commodities that were traded on the Roman stock exchange. And like the Greeks, the ancient Romans designated certain ships for use only in the transport of olive oil. At the same time, the Romans carried olive seedlings to countries bordering the Mediterranean, using the trees as a peaceful means of conquering the people. (More on this later in the chapter.)

Today, Italy grows about thirty varieties of olives and, along with Spain, it is one of the world's leading producers of olive oil. You'll learn more about the olives of Italy in Chapter 3.

The Olive Flourishes in the Middle East

As you've already learned, there is a lack of agreement about the origin of the olive tree. Thus, while some experts claim that the olive was born in the Middle East, others say that it spread from Crete to Syria and Palestine. Regardless of the path the olive took, experts agree that the tree was cultivated in the Mideast as early as 3000 BCE.

Anyone who doubts the significance of the olive in the life of ancient Middle Eastern peoples should turn to the Bible. Strong's Exhaustive Concordance, which lists nearly all the words in the Bible, offers a total of 199

The Bible has more to say about the olive tree—its fruit, its wood, and its oil—than about any other tree. In fact, Strong's Exhaustive Concordance lists nearly two hundred biblical references to the olive.

references to olives, olive yards, oil olive, and just oil—which undoubtedly was the oil of the olive. The verse that opened this chapter is just one example. A more familiar reference to the olive is found in Genesis. Even the youngest Bible scholar is familiar with the story of Noah who, after taking shelter in the ark during the Great Flood, sent forth a dove to look for signs of life. The dove brought back an olive branch, which was the symbol of life not only for the Hebrews, but for many cultures.

As recorded in the Bible, the history of Palestine (now Israel) began with the Jews' journey to the Promised Land. But even when the traveling ark was built by the Israelites in the desert on the way to their new home, olive oil was specified as the oil to use for the lighting of the eternal lamp. According to the Bible, olives were cultivated in the land that would become Israel even before the settlement of the Israelites. In fact, the Jewish people consider olives one of the seven "native" fruits with which the land of Israel is blessed, and to this day, the olive is a popular motif in Jewish art.

By 1000 BCE, the Hebrew kingdom was well established, with Jerusalem as its capital. Saul, the first King of Israel, was anointed with olive oil when he was crowned king. Later, both King Solomon and King David placed great importance on the olive tree, and King David even had guards watch over the olive groves and warehouses to insure the safety of the trees and their precious oils. In fact, *Olea europaea* held such an honored place in the life of the ancients that Moses excused olive growers from military service.

The olive tree has played a part in many events in the Holy Land. As everyone knows, before his arrest, Jesus spent the night in the Garden of Gethsemane at the foot of the Mount of Olives. Many believe that eight of the original olive trees in the Garden of Gethsemane are still in existence. In his book *Sinai and Palestine in Connection With Their History*, historian Arthur Penrhyn Stanley wrote:

In ancient times, oil was extracted from the fruit of the olive tree by means of a stone mill. Many traditional olive oil producers—not only in the Mideast, but all over the world—still use a stone press to make their golden oil.

The eight aged olive trees . . . are now indeed less striking in the modern garden enclosure built around them than when they stood free and unprotected on the rough hillside, but they will remain so long as their already protracted life is spared, the most memorable of their race on the surface of the earth. Their gnarled trunks and scanty foliage will always be regarded as the most affecting of the sacred memorials in or about Jerusalem.

Not just the Jews and the Christians, but the Muslims, too, valued and revered the olive. In the Koran, The Prophet Mohammed (570–632 CE), born in the city of Mecca in what today is Saudi Arabia, wrote:

Allah's light is as a lamp kindled from the blessed tree, an olive, of neither the East nor the West, whose oil is of such luminous glow that it seems to shine though no fire has been touched to it.

Incidentally, the oldest Islamic university, still educating Muslims in Tunisia, is named al-Zitouna, or The Olive Tree.

For centuries, the olives of Palmyra—the ancient city of central Syria, said to have been built by Solomon—enjoyed a reputation as being superior fruit throughout the Mideast. In fact, in ancient times, both Syria and Palestine produced olive oil in abundance. Interestingly, though, it appears that for many years, olives and olive oil shipments were under the control of the Philistines, whose small country bordered the Mediterranean.

One of the reasons the olive tree has long been valued in the Middle East is that it can survive in poor soil that is not hospitable to other types of plants. Today, olives continue to flourish not only in Israel and Syria, but also in a number of other Middle Eastern countries, including Egypt, Iran, Jordan, Lebanon, and Libya.

Although every country of the Middle East has its own distinctly different cuisine, a few foods are common to all Mideastern fare. Among these is the olive.

The Olive Travels to Spain

Although no one knows precisely when the olive tree was first cultivated in Spain, it is known that the Romans expanded Spain's cultivation of the olive and improved production techniques. Today, Spain is the leading producer—and largest exporter—of olive oil.

Many experts believe that the Phoenicians introduced olive cultivation to Spain around 1050 BCE. But it was the Romans, sometime around 45 BCE, who established the lush groves Spain is known for even today. First, olives occupied a stretch in southern Spain, across the Baetica valley. Then the plant spread towards the central region of Spain and to the coastal area of the Iberian Peninsula, moving into Portugal, as well. According to information found in the excavations of Monte Testaccio, over a period of 260 years, Rome imported over 6 billion liters of olive oil, 85 percent of which was produced in southern Spain.

Spain's production of olives and olive oil continued to increase during the occupation of the Moors, which extended from the eighth century to the fifteenth century. Indeed, the Moors are believed to have brought their own varieties of olives with them to the south of Spain, and had such a marked influence on the cultivation of olives in this region that the Spanish words for olive (*aceituna*) and oil (*aceite*), as well as the Portuguese words for olive (*azeitona*) and olive oil (*azeite*), all have Arabic roots.

Today, it is estimated that 215 million olive trees grow in Spain, covering over 5,000,000 acres. It is not surprising that Spain is now the world's leading producer of olive oil.

France Joins in the Harvest

Like the Spanish, the French are indebted to Rome for their olive trees. Under Roman rule, olive groves flourished throughout southern France. And although trade in olive oil temporarily ceased with the fall of the Roman Empire, olive cultivation continued as an important part of French life.

Like many other cultures, French culture includes a legend about the olive. It seems that in 481 CE, the crowning of Clovis I, King of the Franks,

was delayed because no anointing oil was available. According to the story, the coronation took place only when a dove appeared carrying a flask of olive oil. That flask, which was used to store the holy oil that anointed thirty-four French monarchs, now has a home in the Cathedral of Saint-Remy.

The French began keeping records of their olive trees in 1739, and by the mid-1950s, the Roman's ancient plantings had given life to around 20 million trees. During the fierce winter of 1956, however, a million of the sturdy trees froze and died, and 6 million mature trees were severely injured. At that time, disheartened French farmers ripped out dead and dying olive trees, including some that might have returned to life, to make room for grapevines. Since the early 1990s, though, olives and olive oil have been enjoying increasing popularity, and many growers have replaced their grapes with olive trees. France's olive oil is counted among the world's best.

In 1956, a bitter winter devastated the olive groves of France. Spurred by increasing demands, however, French growers continue to plant new olive trees and to produce table olives and oils of superb quality.

The Olive Tree Continues to Spread Its Roots

Before we leave the olive groves of the Old World, it should be noted that the olive tree eventually travelled far beyond the areas where it originated. In the past few hundred years, the growth of the olive has spread to Japan, China, South Africa, and even Australia. Nevertheless, at this time, more than 90 percent of the world's olive oil comes from the Mediterranean region, where it all started.

The New World

On the heels of the conquistadors, olive seedlings were introduced to the American continent, where Franciscan monks carried seeds and cuttings to Mexico, Chile, Argentina, and, finally, California. At the same time, olives also travelled to the West Indies.

In the 1760s, the first cuttings were planted in California at the Mission San Diego de Alcalá, establishing groves that exist to this day. Gradually, the olive trees moved up the coast by way of the missions. By the late 1800s, commercial cultivation had begun in the valleys of central and northern California. Over time, new varieties, imported from both Spain and Italy, improved the quality of the crop.

At first, California's olive trees were valued because of the demand for olive oil. Indeed, by 1885, the oil of California's olives ranked with the world's best. But later, the growers became more interested in the olives themselves. In fact, by the beginning of the twenty-first century, over 90 percent of California's crop was devoted to the production of ripe black olives. In Chapter 3, you'll learn more about the olive groves of the United States.

The olive tree has been carried far and wide since it was first discovered by the ancients. This is not difficult to understand as the olive tree offers so much, from its beautiful wood to its succulent fruit to its luscious oil. In addition, the tree itself is nearly indestructible; if the top dies, a new trunk will often spring from the roots. If you find this fact intriguing, you'll be delighted to know that Chapter 2 offers a closer look at the plant that has fascinated so many people for thousands of years. It then shows how the fruit of this wonderful tree is harvested and, ultimately, transformed into the products that reach your table.

From**Tree** to**Table**

I have exceedingly at heart the introduction
of the olive into Carolina & Georgia, being convinced
it is one of the most precious productions of nature
and contributes the most to the happiness of mankind . . .

—THOMAS JEFFERSON, 1789

As you learned in Chapter 1, olive trees were first cultivated through-out the Mediterranean and Mideast, and then were transported all over the world. Over the years, the olive tree has been valued for its medicinal properties, its edible fruit and oil, its beautiful wood, and so much more. This chapter will familiarize you with this ancient plant, from its gnarled trunk to its feather-shaped leaves. Most impor-tant, you'll learn about the fruit of the tree and discover how it's processed to yield the products that play such an important part in cuisines the world over.

The gnarled branching pattern of the olive tree is quite distinctive, with older trees boasting fantastically shaped trunks that appear to have been supernaturally sculpted.

OLEA EUROPAEA

The olive tree, more formally known as *Olea europaea,* is an evergreen that likes sun and well-drained soil and flourishes in many of the hot, dry areas of the world.

A pretty tree with numerous branches, *Olea europaea* usually reaches a height of twenty to twenty-five feet, but can grow as tall as fifty feet with a spread of about thirty feet. The pale gray bark of the gnarled and twisted trunk covers a beautifully-grained yellowish wood that is prized by cabinetmakers. The lance-shaped leaves, glossy green above and silvery gray below, grow in pairs.

Olive trees bloom in late spring. The small, fragrant, creamy white flowers grow in loose clusters, and are largely hidden by the plant's leaves. These flowers are of two types. Perfect flowers contain both male and female parts, and are capable of developing into olive fruits. Staminate flowers, on the other hand, contain only the pollen-producing parts. Olive trees are wind-pollinated.

The olive fruit is classified as a drupe, similar to plums, cherries, apricots, and peaches. As such, the olive has a single hard stone that encloses one or two seeds. When young, the fruit is green, but it darkens as it ripens, usually turning a blackish purple or even a matte black when fully ripe, although some varieties remain green or turn a copper brown.

The size of the olive ranges from half an inch to a full two inches. The shape of the fruit, too, can vary. While some olives are round, others are oval, and still others are greatly elongated with pointed ends.

The fruit production of an olive tree is often erratic. In some areas, especially where irrigation and fertilization are not practiced, trees bear in alternate years. A tree may have a heavy crop one year, and not even bloom the next.

The Beauty of the Olive Tree

Graceful and billowing, with greenish gray foliage, the olive tree has inspired any number of artists to immortalize its splendor. Here are a few examples of famous painters whose work celebrates the beauty of the olive tree.

❑ Just a year before his death, Vincent van Gogh (1853–1890) wrote to his beloved brother Theo, "If you could see the olives at this moment. The old silver foliage and the silver-green against the blue. And the orange-hued turned earth. . . . It is too beautiful for me to try to conceive of it, or dare to paint it." So van Gogh wrote; yet, in the end, he did dare. Several of his works feature olive trees.

❑ Pierre Auguste Renoir (1814–1919), one of the great French impressionists, moved to Provence, France in 1890. There he discovered anew the beauty of the olive. He wrote, "Look at the light on the olives. It sparkles like diamonds. It is pink, it is blue, and the sky that plays across them is enough to drive you mad." In paintings such as *Olive Garden*, Renoir depicted the olive glowing with pink against silvery trunks. In his later years, Renoir bought an olive grove in Nice just in time to save the majestic trees from being cut down and sold. Later, Renoir built a house on the property.

❑ Paul Cezanne (1839–1906), a contemporary of Renoir, excelled at painting landscapes of his native Provence. Look closely at his works, and you'll see olive trees shadowed against a far-off Mont Sainte-Victoire.

❑ Henri Matisse (1869–1954), a leader of the fauvist movement, featured simple forms and vivid colors in his paintings. One of the earliest works in this style was Promenade Among the Olive Trees, a painting created on the Mediterranean coast. Later in his career, Matisse produced the stunning serigraph Pasiphae Embracing an Olive Tree.

Although commercial growers most value the tree for its fruit, olive trees are often grown solely for their graceful beauty. Whether cultivated for profit or pleasure, the trees are long-lived, with a life expectancy of five hundred years or more. They can survive and bear fruit well even when neglected, showing a titanic resistance that makes them nearly immortal. In fact, if the top dies or the tree is chopped to the ground, a new trunk will often arise from its roots. Perhaps that's why the olive is a symbol of life in so many cultures.

GROWING OLIVES

The hardiness of the olive tree is legendary. Trees that are chopped to the ground often return to life. And although fruit production suffers from climatic extremes, the tree can endure winter freezes and even long periods of drought.

Considering the olive tree's birth in the heat of the Mediterranean and the Middle East, it's not surprising to learn that the tree prefers a region that provides long, hot growing seasons to ripen the fruit, and no late spring frosts, as these can kill the blossoms. The olive tree may be grown as an ornamental, though, where winter temperatures do not drop below 12°F. Where winters are harsher, the tree may be grown in a container and moved indoors when temperatures drop. (You'll learn more about this in Chapter 5.)

Although the fruit of the olive tree contains seeds, the cultivated varieties are never propagated by seed, as the resulting plants revert to the original small-fruit wild varieties. Instead, olives are generally propagated by cuttings, either by hardwood cuttings set in the spring, or by small, leafy cuttings rooted under mist sprays in a propagating frame. Propagation can also be achieved through budding or grafting onto seedling rootstocks. The olive tree begins bearing fruit within four to eight years, but full production is not reached for up to thirty-five years.

Proper pruning is an important part of olive tree cultivation, as it both controls production and shapes the tree for easier harvesting. Usually, it is desirable to limit the tree's height to twenty feet. Olive trees are generally pruned in the spring or early summer, when the plant is in flower.

Where summers are dry, olive trees usually require irrigation. This is especially important when the trees are cultivated on flat land near the sea. Because the leaves of the tree are small, with a protective cuticle and slow transpiration, this hardy plant can survive even extended spells of dry weather. However, when the fruit is in its early stages of growth, a lack of water can cause the olives to be smaller and the oil content to be lower, and may even cause the fruit to fall from the tree.

Commercial growers generally fertilize their olive crops. In California, farmers systematically apply fertilizers each year, well ahead of the time the plants flower. In the Mediterranean, though, many farmers prefer to use organic fertilizers such as dung every other year.

Although the olive tree can be affected by some pests and diseases, it has far fewer problems than most fruit trees. Those pests that can damage the tree vary according to region. In California, for instance, farmers are most concerned about the fungal disease called verticillium wilt. In the Mediterranean, danger is posed by the medfly and the olive fruit fly, the latter of which has been known to destroy entire crops. Olive lovers around the world should be happy to learn that because the olive has fewer natural enemies than many other plants, and because the odor of chemical treatments tends to be retained in the oil of the fruit, the olive is one of the least sprayed crops.

Because the olive tree has fewer natural enemies than most plants—and because the oil of the fruit so readily absorbs the odor of chemical treatments—the olive is one of the least sprayed commercial crops.

HARVESTING OLIVES

The time at which the fruit of the olive tree is harvested is determined partly by whether the fruit is destined for oil production or table olives. When olives are intended for curing, they are usually harvested well before they are ripe. The initial harvest for green olives starts in mid-September, when the fruit is just beginning to show a little color. When black table olives are desired, of course, the fruit is generally picked later in the year—although California "ripe" olives are harvested early in the season and turn black as the result of special processing.

Olives bruise easily, especially when ripe, and must be handled with care. For this reason, traditional farmers handpick their crops rather than harvesting them mechanically.

When olives are intended for oil production—as are the majority of olives cultivated around the world—the fruit is allowed to mature, often remaining on the tree until November or December, when oil yield is optimal. Within this general framework, though, other factors come into play as well, as the precise time at which the olive is picked affects the character of the oil produced. Olives harvested relatively early tend to produce a peppery oil with a full-bodied aroma, for instance, while olives harvested late produce a milder oil. Many growers claim that olives are best harvested for oil when they are three-quarters black, and produce an oil with a pleasing bouquet and low acidity.

Olives may be picked either by hand or by machine. Generally, olives destined for curing are hand harvested to reduce damage to the fruit through bruising. With this method, the fruit is dislodged using a cupped, gloved hand or a plastic hand rake or comb. The olives are then allowed to fall into a ground net or a large piece of fabric. It can take two people from two hours to a half a day to harvest all of the fruit from one olive tree.

Olives cultivated for oil production, as well as some table olives grown on large acreages, are often harvested by machines, which literally shake the fruit off the trees. Like hand-harvested fruit, machine-harvested olives are caught by nets. Naturally, this method greatly lowers labor costs. On traditional farms, however, even olives grown for their oil are handpicked.

Once the olives have been harvested, care must still be taken to protect them. This is especially true of black olives, which bruise easily. Whether the fruit is black or green, though, mold can be a problem between picking and processing, making olives a delicate commodity. Generally, the fruit is transported in baskets or other ventilated containers and then stored in cool, dark areas. Handling is minimized, and processing—whether into oil or table olives—is accomplished as quickly as possible, sometimes within just a few hours of picking.

CURING OLIVES

Whether olives are harvested young and green or ripe and black, when raw, they are not only hard but also bitter due to oleuropein, a foul-tasting gluocoside. The curing process both removes this unpalatable substance and softens the olive, leaving it pleasingly tender.

Raw olives can be processed in several ways. Some of the most popular methods include curing in pure water; curing in brine, a mixture of water and salt or vinegar and salt; and curing in lye. Olives can even be dry-cured using only salt. When brine or other solutions are used as a curative agent, the liquid is usually changed a number of times until all of the bitterness has been leached out of the fruit. Naturally, curing solutions that contain lye are carefully washed from the olives through a series of cold water rinses until no residue remains on the fruit.

The chosen curing method does, of course, affect the flavor of the final product, and different cultures prefer different curing processes. In Sicily, for instance, olives are most often cured in brine, while in the United States, olives are processed in lye, after which a flow of air is used to produce the rich dark color characteristic of California's black olives. In Chapter 3, you'll learn more about the olives produced around the world, and in Chapter 6, you'll find instructions for curing your own olives at home.

Once all bitterness has been removed from the olives, the now-mellow morsels are often preserved in a salty brine or in oil, which may be flavored with herbs and spices such as oregano, thyme, pepppercorns, and coriander seed. Flavorings such as orange and lemon peel may also be added. And, as you'll find just by walking through the aisles of your local supermarket, pitted olives are often enhanced with stuffings of pimento, garlic, almonds, or even anchovies.

Because olives are hard and bitter when picked, they cannot be eaten fresh off the tree. The curing process is designed to leach out the bitterness and transform the fruit into tender, luscious morsels.

The earliest method of curing olives used salt. But by the time of Homer, the Greeks had begun to experiment with different ways of sweetening and softening the fruit of the olive tree.

PRESSING OLIVES TO MAKE OIL

Although hundreds of thousands of tons of table olives are produced each year, a full 90 percent of all commercially grown olives are used to make olive oil. Olives are extremely rich in oils. Six months after olive blossoms first appear on a tree, an olive is 20 to 40 percent oil by weight. Yet it takes eight to ten pounds of fresh olives to produce two pounds of virgin olive oil.

To express the oil from the fruit, olives are first crushed to a paste. Nowadays, this can be done in a number of ways. When a *metal toothed grinder* is used, olives are fed into a toothed grinder which pulverizes the olives. A *hammer mill* has swinging arms that, through centrifugal action, push the olives into the sides of a rotating chamber, which is similar to a home garbage disposal. In a *rotor and screen grinder,* olives are pushed into the gap between the screen and the rotor until the abraded particles pass through the screen. An *eccentric chamber and rotor* pulls olives into a narrowing chamber, where they are squeezed into a paste. Traditional olive oil producers, though, still use a *stone olive mill*—a stone roller or wheel that is moved in circles on a granite slab, grinding the olives into a paste.

Once the olives have been milled, the paste is spread onto round double-layered natural fiber mats with holes in the center. A great many of the mats are stacked onto a platform over a steel pillar. A plate, driven by hydraulic power, then compresses the mats, causing the oil to run out into tubs.

Unfortunately for the olive-oil maker, the oil that flows into the tubs isn't pure; it's mixed with a blackish watery substance that must be separated out. Everyone knows that oil and water don't mix. The vegetable water sinks to the bottom and the oil floats to the top. In the old days, millers scooped the golden oil from the top, resulting in a product that was cloudy rather than clear, but that retained all the delicate flavor of the fruit. Today, though, centrifugal force is used to separate the oil from the water. In

Technology has made it possible to crush the olive in a variety of ways. Traditional olive oil producers, though, still use a stone mill to grind the fruit into a paste.

a fully mechanized plant, where up to 11,000 pounds of olives are pressed a day, the watery oil is put into a huge vat with a drain at the bottom, and the mixture is allowed to settle. As the oil rises to the top, its weight pushes some of the water down the drain. The liquid, still full of vegetable water and bits of olive pulp, is then mechanically pumped into a tank situated above a stainless steel centrifugal spinner. Hot water is pumped into the spinner, followed by the oily liquid. When the machine is set spinning, pure oil is thrown out one pipe, while waste water drains out the other.

Obviously, the modern method of separating olive oil from vegetable water is much easier and more profitable than the traditional technique, and is now the most common way of processing oil. But there are those who say that mixing hot water with the oil in the centrifuge washes away a lot of flavor. In addition, the friction caused by the high-speed spinning is said to alter the composition of the oil. Olive oil processed in a centrifuge is clear and clean, however, and that's the way many people prefer it.

GRADES OF OLIVE OIL

The above discussion provided the basics of olive-oil making. But olives are a valuable commodity, and the process doesn't end when the first oil is pressed from the fruit. Other pressings follow the first, and finally, chemicals are used to extract the last precious drops of oil from the mashed olives. The result of each of these pressings is then graded. Although the grading system categorizes oils according to their acidity, it also reflects the manner in which the oil was removed from the olives. That's why our examination of the olive from tree to table wouldn't be complete without a discussion of the various grades of oil.

It should be noted at this point that the characteristics of any given oil—its color, flavor, aroma, and body—are the result of many factors,

The grade of an olive oil doesn't define the product's taste. But labels such as *extra virgin*, *virgin*, and *pure* are good indications of an oil's body, purity, and quality.

including not only the method of extraction, but also the variety of olives used, the degree of ripeness the olives attained before being pressed, and the climate and soil that nurtured the tree. Therefore, the grade assigned to an oil won't tell you whether a given oil is peppery or buttery, pale yellow or deep green. But it is a good indication of body, purity, and quality.

Extra Virgin Olive Oil

Considered the champagne of oils, extra virgin olive oil is a cold-pressed product made without chemicals. Moreover, this oil is low in acid and rates high in terms of flavor, aroma, and body.

To be labeled *extra virgin*, olive oil must have an acid content of less than one percent, and must rate high in terms of taste, aroma, and body. Extra virgin olive oil is always a cold-pressed product from the first pressing of the fruit, and is free of the chemicals used to extract oils for certain lesser grades. It is considered the finest of all the olive oils, and is priced accordingly. This oil has all the characteristics of the olives from which it was taken. So although it is always full-bodied and fragrant, it can vary widely in flavor, color, and aroma.

The champagne of oils, extra virgin olive oil needs no enhancement and is delicious poured straight on bread, drizzled on salad greens, or tossed into pasta. The full olive taste comes through in every bite.

Virgin Olive Oil

In general, virgin olive oil is milder than extra virgin oil. But many other factors, from the variety of olives being used to the time of the harvest, also affect flavor.

Like extra virgin olive oil, *virgin olive oil* is a product of cold pressing and contains no chemicals. Any olive oils subjected to solvents or other foreign substances to aid extraction cannot legally be labelled "virgin." However, this oil is slightly more acidic than extra virgin products, with up to 2 percent acidity. In addition, virgin oil doesn't rate as high as extra virgin products in terms of taste, aroma, and body, and may be pressed from fruits that are not the highest in quality. Although its flavor varies in intensity, virgin olive oil is generally milder than extra virgin oil.

For many years, virgin olive oil was the standard in this country, and it's still a very fine choice. Use this oil anytime you want good olive flavor—in salad dressings, marinades, and dipping sauces.

Pure Olive Oil

Pure olive oil is a mixture of refined oil and virgin or extra virgin oil, the latter of which is added for flavor and aroma. It does not include lampante oil (described below), and has an acid level of no more than 1.5 percent.

Lower in quality than extra virgin and virgin products, pure olive oil is a mixture of chemically treated refined oils and virgin or extra virgin oils.

Because the refined olive oil used in this product has been chemically treated and filtered to correct its taste and lower its acidity, the quality of pure olive oil is not as high as that of virgin oils. Thus, while it is a perfectly acceptable oil that is used happily around the world, discriminating olive lovers generally use this relatively bland product only for frying. In fact, since the flavor of extra virgin olive oil tends to break down at frying temperatures, pure olive oil—which is often simply labelled *olive oil*—is frequently recommended as the olive oil of choice for frying.

Lampante

The mash that is left after oil is extracted from the first pressing of olives is called pomace. When this mash is pressed again with the addition of hot water, the resulting high-acid oil is called *lampante* because of its ancient use as lamp oil. Lampante must be further refined to remove excess acid, color, and odor. Sold commercially as *refined olive oil* or *commercial olive oil,* lampante is used primarily for blending with first-press oil to produce a good tasting edible oil. It is not marketed directly to the consumer.

Other Olive Oils

The above discussion reviewed the most common grades of olive oil. But when shopping in your supermarket or specialty store, you may well see products that are labelled with designations other than those mentioned above. In fact, the array of olive oils now available is truly dizzying!

A number of olive oils are now described by the term *fine* or *fino* (*fino* means "fine" in Italian). These products are simply blends of extra virgin and virgin olive oils, making them suitable for use in salads and cooking. The acid level of fino olive oils varies widely, ranging from 1 to 3 percent.

In recent years, yet another product called *light olive oil* has appeared in supermarkets. Contrary to what many consumers believe, this oil has neither fewer calories nor less fat than its "heavier" counterparts. Rather, the product is lighter in both color and fragrance than other olive oils, and also has little of the classic olive oil flavor. The advantage of light olive oil is twofold. First, its bland flavor makes it perfect for baking and cooking whenever a distinctive olive taste would be undesirable. Second, the filtration process used to create light oil gives it a higher smoke point than regular olive oil, making it suitable even for deep-frying.

> Light olive oils are lighter than regular oils in color, flavor, and odor—not in calories. Relatively bland, these oils are perfect for use in cake, cookie, and muffin batters.

Finally, we come to the *flavored olive oils.* Available in gourmet shops everywhere, these products have been infused with garlic, lemon, roasted peppers, basil, or a combination of ingredients. Used alone, a drizzle of these oils perks up the blandest vegetables, while a bowlful makes a great dipping sauce or marinade. Or add a bit of vinegar to the flavored oil of your choice to create an instant salad dressing.

Despite the fact that olives must be painstakingly cured or carefully pressed into a luscious oil before being enjoyed, this legendary fruit is cultivated on six continents. Perhaps you are already aware of the many wonderful olive products that now are available. If, however, you still can't tell a mellow Mission olive from a rich Kalamata, turn the page, and begin your personal tour of the world of olives.

CHAPTER 3

Olives of the World

For what it symbolizes, first of all—
peace with its leaves and joy with its golden oil.

—ALDOUS HUXLEY (1894–1963)

Olives are found flourishing on six continents. Remarkably, there are more than 700 varieties of olives under cultivation. If you are not yet sufficiently impressed by the extent of olive cultivation, consider this: Estimates indicate that there are 800 million fruit-bearing olive trees in the world, yielding more than 7.8 million metric tons of fruit per year! Only a fraction of this mammoth yield is reserved for table olives, while 7.2 million metric tons of olives are pressed into golden oil.

These figures demonstrate how country after country, culture after culture, has embraced the olive, cultivating the wondrous tree and enthusias-

Every olive-growing country and culture has devised its own ways of curing olives or of adding marvelous flavor after curing is complete. By sampling different olives, both domestic and imported, you're sure to find the ones that best suit your fancy and satisfy your culinary needs.

tically making use of its luscious fruit. The result is the marvelous array of oils and table olives now available in supermarkets, in specialty stores, in fine restaurants, and even over the Internet. This chapter will take you on a tour of the major olive-producing countries of the world, introducing you to their most important olive products. To help you make a wise selection on the next trip to your gourmet shop, it presents a handy guide to some of the more noteworthy olives available, along with their country of origin and a brief description. And finally, once you've chosen your olive products, this chapter will teach you tried-and-true techniques for keeping them fresh and flavorful.

THE MIDDLE EAST

As you learned in Chapter 1, many experts believe that the olive had its birth in the Middle East. Although some dispute this claim, all agree that the olive tree was cultivated in the Mideast as early as 3000 BCE. These trees continue to flourish, some of them as ancient as the countries in which they are so carefully tended.

A number of Middle Eastern countries are noteworthy for their production of olive oil. Turkey and Syria lead, producing 180,000 and 165,000 metric tons, respectively. (Note that a metric ton is about 2,205 pounds, or 205 pounds heavier than a short ton—the unit of measure used in the United States.) Behind these countries come Palestine, with 20,000 metric tons; Jordan, with 17,000; Lebanon, with 6,000; Israel and Cyprus, with 5,000 each; Libya and Iran, with 3,000 each; and Egypt, with only .5.

Middle Eastern oils come from a variety of olives. In Israel, for instance, the most common olive is the Manzanillo, which produces a smooth, lightly textured oil with a relatively mild flavor. The best, however, is considered the Souri (or Sury)—a small, wonderfully rich-tasting olive that is especially suitable for olive oil because of its aromatic taste and high oil content. Oils made from this olive have a distinctive honey-and-pepper flavor and an herbal aroma. *Souri,* by the way, means "Syrian," and this olive is native not only to Israel but also to much of the Mideast. Other Israeli olive varieties include Barnea, which produces a sweet, lightly fruity olive oil; Nabali, which yields a smooth, mild oil; Santa; and Novo.

Of course, not all olives grown in the Mideast are pressed for their oil. Walk through any market in that region, and tantalizing smells wafting from barrels of both green and ripe olives will set your mouth watering. Olives marinated with coriander, ginger, hot pepper, lemon juice, and thyme, as well as other herbs and spices, simply must be sampled. In many Arab countries, pungent brine-cured ripe olives are a particular favorite. An old Arabian riddle asks, "Our servant is green, but her children are born white and then grow black. Who is she?" The answer, of course, is the olive tree.

Few Middle Eastern olives appear to be available in North America. One of the exceptions are the olives of Israel. There, the best of the firm green olives are cracked and cured in brine with garlic, lemon, and herbs. Luckily for us, some of these luscious morsels are available in specialty shops or through mail order.

Israeli olives are usually cracked before curing. Originally, the cracking was accomplished with stones or wooden mallets. Now, a specially made crank-operated grinder is often used to perform the job quickly and easily.

NORTH AFRICA

In Chapter 1, you learned how the Roman conquerors established lush olive groves in Spain and France. But the spread of olive culture didn't end there, for the Romans carried seedlings all along the countries of the Mediterranean, including those of North Africa. Today, perhaps the most prolific of the olive producers in this region are those of Tunisia and Morocco.

Tunisia

Centrally located on the Mediterranean, not far from the olive groves of Italy, Tunisia is the largest producer of olive oil outside of the European Union, with an average yearly output of 170,000 metric tons. It is estimated that Tunisia has over 56 million olive trees. The predominant variety, the Chemlali, is a close relative of the variety that produces excellent oil in the French Riviera. Other varieties include Zalmati, Chetoui, Meski, and Chaal. Some experts claim that there are as many as a hundred varieties of olive trees in Tunisia.

About 38 percent of Tunisia's oil is extra virgin, the best being a smooth oil with a slight nip, but no bitterness. Most of this oil—about 74 percent—is exported to Italy, while 26 percent of Tunisia's oil goes to Spain, and a mere 2 percent is exported to the United States.

Morocco

Moroccans grow fewer trees than Tunisia and export little oil. The oil that they do produce would not suit Western tastes, being strongly acidic to satisfy the preferences of those who buy it domestically. But the people of Morocco are world champions of table olive production.

Although the country does not cultivate many varieties—most are a hardy version of the French Picholine—experts claim that the Moroccans have devised more than a hundred ways of curing and preserving olives, and each one is distinctive and delectable. In Moroccan markets, tubs are heaped with black dry-cured olives; green olives marinated with fiery red chilies; and purple olives prepared with garlic, parsley, rosemary, and other herbs. In addition to those olives sold domestically, Morocco exports 60,000 tons of olives per year, making it second only to Spain. In fact, Morocco sells much of its crop to Spain, and supplies three-quarters of

France's olives, as well. In the United States, you are most likely to find dry-cured black Moroccan olives. These olives, which have a meaty texture akin to that of prunes, are somewhat bitter, and are best used for cooking rather than snacking.

EUROPE

Since the formation of the European Union in the mid-1900s, the International Olive Oil Council no longer reports individual production figures for each of the European countries. Instead, they group together various European countries in which olives and olive oils are highly prized, including Spain, Italy, France, and Greece. And the results are truly staggering. At the beginning of the twenty-first century, the combined olive oil production of these countries was 1,912,000 metric tons of high-quality olive oil!

Although, as you know, the vast majority of olives are grown for their oil, a portion of the crop is also used to make delectable table olives. Let's look at each of these countries and learn about their olive products.

Spain

Today, Spain is the world's leading producer of olive oil, as well as the world's largest exporter of the product. The country boasts over 5 million acres of olive groves, with over 215 million trees. This amounts to over 27 percent of the world's olive production.

Over 90 percent of the olives grown for olive oil in Spain are the Arbequina variety. These olives produce an oil that, at its best, is intensely green, sweet, and fruity, with a wonderful aroma. Other olive varieties used for oil include Picual, Hojiblanca, Lechin, Cornicabra, Verdial, Picudo, and Empeltre. Some are exported as single varietals, while others

The world's leading producer of olive oil, Spain exports oil to over ninety-five countries, including Italy, France, Germany, Portugal, Holland, the United Kingdom, Japan, Australia, Brazil, Canada, and, of course, the United States.

are sold as blends. Because Spain has a surprising variety of climates and microclimates, its oils provide a wide range of aromas and tastes, ranging from light and sweet to slightly bitter and pungent.

Of course, Spain is also known for its superb table olives. The large "super colossal" Sevillano olives are world famous. The Spanish like these big olives pitted and cured with vinegar and salt only, although some are filled with spicy pimentos to give them a little heat. Other olives include the Arbequina, a small round, brown olive with a mild, smoky flavor; the large green Gordal, usually known as "Queen" olives in this country; the slightly smaller, crisper, green Manzanilla; and the sweet black olives known as Farga Aragon or Empeltre.

Italy

Italy is hard on the heels of Spain, growing 26 percent of the world's olives and producing 24 percent of the world's olive oil. All regions of Italy grow olives, with the country cultivating about thirty varieties in all. Some of the better known varieties grown for oil include Frantoio, Leccino, and Moraiolo. Often, blends are made of green and black olives to produce an oil with a distinctive flavor. The best of the oils of Italy are robust and hearty, with a fruity taste and a peppery finish.

Like Spain, in addition to fine oils, Italy produces a selection of excellent table olives. The small black Taggiasca olive, grown in the Italian Riviera, is similar to but slightly bigger and meatier than the French Niçoise, and is usually cured in brine and scented with herbs such as thyme, rosemary, and bay leaves. Purple-brown Gaeta, grown in central Italy, are either dry-cured, which makes them black and wrinkled, or brine-cured, which makes them dark purple and smooth-skinned. And huge Cerignolas, which can be green or black in color, are familiar sights on antipasto platters.

Greece

Greece holds third place among the world's olive producers. Almost 350,000 Greek families are involved in the cultivation of olive trees, and the country boasts one hundred olive varieties, which have been created over the centuries to match local variations in temperature, rainfall, soil, and wind resistance. Many groves are still owned by small farmers who harvest their crop by hand.

Despite the enormous variety of Greek olives, most of the country's oil comes from the Kalamata olive, producing a robust liquid with a pleasing, faintly grassy flavor. Kalamatas are also the best-known Greek table olives. With a distinctive, pointed almond shape and a beautiful black-purple color, these olives undergo a unique curing process. After being cracked, they are cured in a red wine vinegar brine, lending them an almost wine-like taste. Other Greek table olives include Amphissas, purple-black olives that are sweet and meltingly soft-textured; meaty Thasos, wrinkled olives that have been dry-cured and coated with olive oil; Naf-plions, cracked green brine-cured olives with a nutty, slightly smoky flavor; and Elitses, tiny, sweet, black olives from Crete. As you might guess, many more varieties are produced, some of which never make it as far as the United States. Upscale supermarkets and specialty shops often offer "Greek olive medleys," which contain several types of Greek olives packed in a natural brine.

France

France cultivates about 5 million olive trees. While Spain produces about 970,000 tons of olive oil annually; Italy, 420,000 tons; and Greece, 300,000 tons; France is now producing only about 2,400 tons, as it is still recovering from the devastating freeze of 1956. However, production is increasing annually with yearly plantings of new trees, and some French oils are now challenging the best of Tuscany and Sicily.

All French olive oil comes from the region of Provence in southern France, which offers an ideal climate for olive growing. The best of the French oils are subtle, soft, and fruity, with exceptionally low acidity and no bitterness. These oils have only recently become available on the American market.

Because of the popular Salade Niçoise, Americans are more familiar with French olives than they are with the country's olive oil. Sometimes called the jewels of the olive world, tiny black Niçoise olives have a unique somewhat sharp flavor. Other olives of France include the torpedo-shaped, brine-cured green Picholines; the salt-cured black Nyons; and the buttery tasting green Lucques. Not surprisingly, these morsels are often prepared with Provençal olive oils and herbes de Provence—rosemary, thyme, tarragon, basil, savory, fennel, marjoram, and lavender.

AUSTRALIA

It may surprise you to learn that Australia has a thriving olive industry. A brief history reveals that the first olive groves were established in the early 1800s around Sydney. The oldest olive trees in Australia are said to be those growing in the gardens of Parliament House in Perth. During the nineteenth century, nearly all states and territories "down under" were planted with some varieties of olive trees, including trees imported from France, Sicily, and South America. The New Norcia Monastery in Western Australia won a silver medal for its olive oil at the Franco-British Exhibition of 1908.

There was a period of time when Australia exported olive oil to Italy, of all places. Today, the demand for olive oil by Australians exceeds the home-grown supply, and Australia must import both oil and table olives to satisfy its country's needs. Nevertheless, the country is now well on its way to establishing an internationally competitive industry, and now produces about one metric ton of olive oil a year.

Over one hundred known varieties of olives are cultivated in Australia. The most common are the oil varieties Corregiola, Frantoio, Paragon, Picual, and Nevadillo; the Kalamata and Hardy's Mammoth table olives; and the Mission and Manzanillo varieties, which are grown both for oil and table olives. As yet, these are not widely available in North American stores, but can be ordered by mail and over the Internet.

Although Australia is rapidly building an olive industry, domestic need now far exceeds production. Every year, to meet demands at home, the country imports approximately 16,000 tons of olive oil and 7,000 tons of olives.

THE AMERICAS

In Chapter 1, you learned how olive seedlings were introduced to the Americas by Franciscan monks, who carried seeds and cuttings to Mexico, Chile, Argentina, and, finally, California. Although olives continue to grow in all of these regions, the olive industry in California is the most prolific by far.

Central and South America

As previously discussed, olive trees continue to grow in Argentina, Chile, and Mexico. Both Argentina and Mexico report their oil production to the International Olive Oil Council, with Argentina producing about 3,000 metric tons per year, and Mexico producing 1,500 metric tons. These oils are produced using traditional methods, and those who have tasted Mexican olive oil find it to be exceptional, with a full herbal flavor that mellows over time. Unfortunately, problems abound in the olive groves of Central and South America. Many old trees, untended for years, have not been pruned and now are too tall to be properly harvested. Many trees are unwatered. Growers, however, are hopeful for the future, and look forward to a time when better cultivation methods can be implemented and oil becomes available for exportation.

Chile does not report any olive oil production. But, fortunately for olive lovers everywhere, this country both produces and exports delicious table olives. The large Alphonso olive is cured in either a wine or wine vinegar solution, lending it a beautiful dark purple color. The flesh of the Alphonso is wonderfully tender and has a tart, slightly bitter flavor.

California

Few Americans realize that the Great Seal of the United States contains thirteen olive leaves and thirteen olives. These symbols are said to represent the country's wish for peace.

Chapter 1 explained how olive trees travelled northward up the coast of California in the 1700s and 1800s, moving from mission to mission. In the late 1800s, varieties from Spain and Italy were introduced, further enhancing the crop both in quantity and quality. Now, California is the home of 1,200 growers with orchards ranging from 5 to 1,000-plus acres in size. A total of 35,000 acres are under cultivation. California's growers have found that the mild winters and hot dry summers of the San Joaquin and Sacramento Valleys are very much like the climate of the Mediterranean—a perfect place to cultivate the olive tree. And their yield bears out this claim, for the industry processes as many as 160,000 tons of olives a year.

At first, California's olive trees were grown largely for their oil. That changed long ago, however, and now, 90 to 95 percent of the state's crop is processed as canned ripe olives. The remaining olives are made into various specialty olives—Greek- and Sicilian-style olives, for instance—or crushed for olive oil.

From the smallest to the largest, the varieties of olives produced in California include Redding, Picholine, Nevadillo, Mission, Manzanillo,

Barouni, Ascolano, and Sevillano. The most important of these varieties are the Mission, the Manzanillo, the Sevillano, and the Ascolano.

The Mission olive was the variety first cultivated by the Franciscan missions. These mild and mellow olives are almost round in shape and fairly large in size. Most commonly, these olives appear commercially as ripe black olives. However, they are also processed as green ripe olives, Greek-style olives, and Spanish-style green olives, and are even used for oil extraction when oil prices are high.

California's Manzanillo olives account for most of the acreage under cultivation. This oval fruit is a bit larger than the Mission, and also a bit meatier. The Manzanillos are usually sold commercially as green Spanish-style olives, often with stuffings of pimento, garlic, or almonds. These are the olives that are often used in martinis. However, Manzanillos are also processed as black ripe olives, and are sometimes pressed for their oil.

The largest and meatiest of California's olives, the Sevillano commands a premium price in the marketplace. These olives are often processed to make green Spanish-style olives, but are also used to make ripe and Sicilian-style olives.

Only slightly smaller than the Sevillano, the Ascolano olive is also a valued variety, although it is easily bruised during harvesting and processing. The oil content of the Ascolano is high, but since this variety makes such a good table olive, it is usually processed as such, either ripe or green.

Before we leave the groves and canneries of California, it is interesting to note that the so-called "ripe" California olives—the industry's trademark—are not ripe at all. Rather, these olives are picked when still green and then cured with lye, after which a flow of bubbling air turns them a rich dark color. A trace of organic iron salt (ferrous gluconate) is then added to fix the color so that the olives won't fade in the can.

The best-known product of California's olive industry is the California ripe olive—a mellow black olive with a firm texture and mild taste. Surprisingly, this olive is actually picked green and then darkened through a special curing process.

MAKING YOUR SELECTION

If you've been munching on mild domestic olives or using bland vegetable oils all your life, hopefully, this chapter has opened your eyes to the many exciting olives and oils the world has to offer. When purchasing olive oil, you'll probably now opt for a virgin or extra virgin product. Then, over time, you'll discover which particular brand or blend pleases you the most. (To learn how to arrange an olive oil tasting, see the inset on page 44.)

If you're in the market for olives rather than olive oils, you'll find that it's a bit easier to judge an olive by its name than it is to choose an oil by its

OLIVES AT A GLANCE

Variety	Origin	Description
Alphonso	Chile	Cured in either a wine or wine vinegar solution, large, dark purple Alphonsos are tender with a tart flavor.
Amphissa	Greece	These purple-black olives are meaty and sweet. Great for snacking, the Amphissa is, unfortunately, hard to find in the United States.
Arbequina	Spain	Mild, with a slightly smoky flavor, these tiny olives are wonderful but a bit hard to find in the United States.
Ascolano	U.S.	Slightly smaller than the Sevillano, this olive is processed either green or ripe.
Cerignola	Italy	If you're lucky enough to find these Italian delights, you'll enjoy a taste of Italy. Both the black and green Cerignolas are large and mild, with a smoky-sweet flavor. Good snacking indeed.
Elitses	Greece	Tiny and sweet, these black olives are hard to find in the United States, but well worth the search.
Farga Aragon	Spain	These succulently sweet black olives are almond shaped and, at their best, very delicious. Unfortunately, they are not well known in the United States.
Gaeta or Empeltre	Italy	These small black olives are either dry-cured in salt, leaving them wrinkled, or brine-cured, making them smooth. Gaeta are intensely flavorful, but watch out for the pits.
Gordal or Queen	Spain	Often known as Queen olives in this country, Spanish Gordals are large and green, with a firm meaty texture.
Kalamata	Greece	Picked when ripe, these fleshy black olives—rich but mild—are cured in red wine vinegar. Eat Kalamata olives out of hand or toss them into salads.
Lucques	France	Tender Lucques have an almost buttery flavor. An exotic choice to tempt guests who say they don't care for olives, Lucques make a mild tapenade that's always a hit.

label. As you've learned, certain varieties of olives processed in certain ways have specific characteristics. But perhaps you're now overwhelmed by all the different olives, and you're at a loss as to which ones have the characteristics you're looking for—mild or pungent, sweet or sharp, firm or soft. If so, the following table may help. Each listing provides the country of origin and offers a hint of the olive's flavor and, in some cases, its culinary uses. Of course, the proof is in the eating, and ultimately you'll have to sample a few varieties to find the ones you like best. But this table should guide you in homing in on those that would best suit your fancy.

Variety	Origin	Description
Manzanilla	Spain	Green, sweet, and crisp in texture, these medium-sized olives are served alongside a glass of sherry in southern Spain.
Manzanillo	U.S.	Often used in martinis, this large green olive is usually prepared Spanish-style with a stuffing of pimento, garlic, or almonds.
Mission	U.S.	Mission olives are old friends. These are the black olives you find everywhere, including the tops of salads and pizzas. Flavorful but mild, they make an inexpensive base for tapenade.
Nafplions	Greece	These green, brine-cured olives are somewhat salty, with a nutty flavor.
Niçoise	France	Often packed with herbs, black Niçoise olives have a distinctive sharp taste. They are indispensable in Salade Niçoise, and excellent for tapenade.
Nyons	France	First dry-cured and then aged in brine, black Nyons are plump and wrinkled, with a rich flavor. They're hard to find, though.
Picholine	France	Brine-cured, with a salty-sweet flavor and solid flesh, torpedo-shaped green Picholines are good for munching with your favorite beverage. If imported, expect them to be marinated in herbes de Provence.
Sevillano	Spain and U.S.	These large green olives are mild but flavorful, and make impressive additions to buffet tables. You'll often find Spanish Sevillanos stuffed with pimento.
Sicilian	Sicily	Large greenish-brown Sicilian olives are brine-cured and have a mild flavor with a tart finish. U.S.-made Sicilian-style olives—which are easier to find—are good for snacking and make a fine tapenade.
Taggiasca	Italy	This small, brine-cured black olive is rich in oil, and similar to but bigger than the Niçoise olive of France. The Taggiasca is often scented with thyme, rosemary, and bay leaves.
Thasos or Throumbes	Greece	These shriveled dry-cured olives have an intense flavor and a meaty texture. Grown on the island of Thasos, they are also known as Throumbes.

Hold Your Own Olive Oil Tasting

Although this chapter provides only a glimpse of the many olive oils produced worldwide, it's clear that the variety of available oils is enormous. There are Italian oils, French oils, and even Australian oils; shimmering green oils and pale yellow oils; single-varietal oils and blends. Even if you limit yourself to the cream-of-the-crop extra virgin products, you will be confronted with a dizzying array of choices.

How can you tell which oil will best please your palate? While the descriptions provided in this chapter are a good starting place, there's no way to tell without opening a bottle and tasting the oil for yourself. That's what professional oil tasters do. Whether determining trade classifications for the marketplace or rating oils in competitions, these individuals use a proven protocol to judge each product. Of course, professional tasters are selected for their sensitive palates and are carefully trained to detect specific attributes. But by sampling oils in a systematic way, you will develop a more sensitive palate over time. And along the way, you're sure to find some truly luscious products—oils that can be used in many of your favorite dishes, or can simply be poured on bread whenever you want to savor the sophisticated olive.

How Do You Set Up an Olive Oil Tasting?

As you're not a professional olive oil taster, try to make your tastings as much fun as possible. Invite friends to share the experience, and turn it into an occasion. At the same time, to get the truest impressions possible of each product, you'll want to follow these guidelines:

❏ For at least thirty minutes before the tasting, avoid sweets, coffee, and any strong-tasting foods that can affect your senses of taste and smell. Also avoid the use of perfumes, deodorants, and lipstick.

❏ Limit the number of samples to three or four per sitting, as it is difficult to accurately judge more oils than this. Choose extra virgin oils—not refined oils whose flavors and pigments have been removed during processing. Make sure that the oils are at room temperature.

❏ Because an initial overpowering oil can cause all subsequent oils to taste stronger than they are, screen the oils by their aroma to decide the order in which they should be tasted, placing the milder oils first, and the more intense oils last.

❏ Pour about a tablespoon of each olive oil sample into a small tasting glass. Taking one sample at a time, rotate the glass to wet the sides, and warm it in your hands. Then inhale deeply, noting the characteristics. (You'll learn more about this later in the inset.)

❏ For the actual tasting, either take a small sip of each oil in turn, or spread the oil on unsalted white bread or a chunk of cold boiled potato. (Experts claim that boiled potato is the better choice, as bread subtly alters the taste of the oil.) If sipping the oil, be sure to distribute it throughout the entire mouth cavity. Then, with your lips partially closed, inhale rapidly two or three times to mix air with the oil on your tongue. First, note the feel of the oil. Is it light or heavy, pleasant or oily? Then, note the flavor. Finally, spit the oil out.

❏ Between samples, drink lots of water to cleanse your palate. Also try chewing a slice of apple or eating a small piece of bread, rinsing again before sampling the next oil.

What Are You Looking For?

Experienced olive oil tasters can distinguish a multitude of good and bad characteristics. During your tastings, though, try to look for just a few major good and bad features.

Positive Characteristics

Almond. An almond aftertaste associated with sweet oils.

Bitterness. A good trait in moderation, this should be transient.

Fruitiness. A flavor and aroma similar to that of a mature olive.

Harmonious. A well-balanced blending of all the qualities of the oil.

Pungency. A rough, burning, biting, or peppery sensation felt in the back of the throat.

Negative Characteristics

Earthy. A taste or smell resulting from soiled, unwashed fruit.

Musty. A moldy flavor resulting from overly long storage of olives before pressing.

Rancid. A rank, disagreeable odor or taste, this is considered the worst defect of all.

Rough. A thick, pasty, or greasy mouth feel.

Winey. A highly acidic taste.

The first few times you sample oils, don't be discouraged if you can't discern all the different characteristics—and don't be afraid to use your own terms to describe your own personal experience. Over time, you will find the oils that suit you best.

One last note is in order regarding your next olive-seeking mission. As you'll learn by glancing through the table on pages 42 to 43—or by strolling through your local supermarket or specialty store—many of these olives are difficult to find. The canned and packaged olives you'll see in your supermarket usually include the large Spanish Sevillanos, often stuffed with pimentos or almonds; the Spanish "Queen" (Gordal) olives; California's green Manzanillos and black Missions; and Greece's ever-popular Kalamatas. You will probably have more luck in the deli section of the market or in your specialty store, as many of them display loose olives marinated in oils and herbs, dry-cured olives, and Greek olive medleys. But buttery French Lucques and tiny Greek Elitses may prove elusive.

Fortunately, a number of mail-order companies now carry a variety of marvelously exotic olives. The Resource List on page 185 will guide you to several companies with tempting offerings. And if you have Internet access, a quick search—either for olives in general or for a particular variety—is sure to turn up more sources of both olives and luscious olive oils.

STORING OLIVES AND OLIVE OILS

When storing leftover olives—whether store-bought or homemade—be sure to cover the olives completely with the brine. An excellent preservative, brine helps prevent spoilage.

Both olives and olive oils have a relatively long shelf life. No food lasts forever, though, and after you've purchased your favorite olive products, you'll want to take the simple steps necessary to keep these precious foods fresh and delicious until you're ready to use them.

Unopened olives, preserved in cans or jars, can be stored at room temperature for up to two years. Once the olives have been opened, though, refrigerate them in their own liquid in a nonmetal container, and most varieties will remain fresh for two or three weeks. Leftover California ripe olives, however, should be stored for ten days at most. Avoid keeping these olives in an airtight container, as harmful toxins may develop. Instead, cover the top with plastic wrap to allow oxygen to permeate the contents.

Although it may be tempting to save money by buying the extra-large container of olive oil, it's far better to buy the oil in smaller sizes. Another option is to buy in bulk and then decant the oil into smaller containers, preferably choosing a can or a dark-colored bottle to protect the oil from light. Keep in mind, too, that oil will quickly absorb any flavors or odors remaining in containers, so it's important to use bottles or cans that are scrupulously clean. For the same reason, avoid storing your oil in a plastic container, as the oil can absorb PVCs.

Light, heat, and air are the enemies of oil, and can turn your purchase rancid. Try to store your oil in an airtight container away from the light, and in a cool place—about 57°F, which is the same temperature as a wine cellar. As a matter of fact, a wine cellar is a great place to store your olive oil.

There is no need to refrigerate your olive oil. Doing so will cause your oil to turn cloudy—although it will not affect its flavor. Fortunately, any oil that's clouded over will clear once it's been warmed to room temperature.

Properly stored, extra virgin olive can be stored for up to two years, although its flavor is usually best when consumed within one year. Lesser-quality olive oils, such as the "pure" oils common on supermarket shelves, tend to spoil more rapidly due to their higher levels of acidity.

This chapter has examined many different olives and olive oils, focusing on the unique flavor that each product has to offer. But, as you well know, there's more to the olive than its appealing taste. In the last few years, study after study has demonstrated the health benefits of the olive. This is nothing new, though. Various parts of the olive tree have been used as medicinals since ancient times. So turn to the next chapter and read about the olive and your health.

Air, heat, and light can turn your precious olive oil rancid. To keep your oil fresh and flavorful, store it in an airtight container and keep the container in a cool, dark place.

CHAPTER 4

Olives, Health, and Beauty

And with the sprig of a fruited olive,
man is purified in extreme health.

—VIRGIL (70–19 BCE)

It may surprise you to learn that Virgil, the Roman poet who is best known for his epic work *Aeneid,* was the son of a prosperous farmer. He not only received an excellent classical education, but was also thoroughly grounded in agriculture, and in his early life, spent a good deal of time overseeing the cultivation and harvesting of the family's olive groves. When he wrote the words that open this chapter, Virgil was expressing what was then a universally accepted truth. Olives and olive oil were not only staples of the Roman diet, but also part and parcel of the pharmacy of the day.

More than two thousand years later, we're still praising the health benefits of the olive—not just the fruit, but also the leaf. This chapter will first take a brief look at the historical use of the olive to preserve and restore well-being. It will then examine what medical experts today know about the wholesome and healthful olive. And finally, it will look at the many ways in which the olive can be used to enhance beauty.

A HISTORICAL OVERVIEW

The health benefits of the olive have been recognized for millennia. Over two thousand years ago, Hippocrates, the Father of Medicine, called olive oil "the great therapeutic."

As already mentioned, the ancient Romans placed great value on the health properties of the olive. And they were by no means the only ancients to do so. The Greek physician Hippocrates (c. 460–377 BCE), the Father of Medicine, repeatedly referred to the curative powers of olive oil, calling it "the great therapeutic." Both the Greeks and the Romans used the fruit, oil, and leaves of the olive tree to keep skin and muscles supple, to cleanse and heal wounds, and to repair the burning and drying effects of sun and water.

The ancient Chinese, too, employed the healing olive in a variety of ways—and practitioners of traditional Chinese medicine continue to do so today. According to the Chinese *Materia Medica*, the ancient reference on Chinese herbal medicine, olives are associated with autumn, a time when nature is drying seeds and moving sap to the roots. This may explain why the Chinese saw olives as having astringent properties and used it to stop the flow of blood from hemorrhoids, to treat a bleeding stomach, and to cure diarrhea and dysentery. Olives, both cured and fresh, were also used by the Chinese to relieve a sore throat, a chronic cough, and even alcoholism.

As the olive spread from the Old World to the New, new cultures discovered its healthful properties. *The Dispensatory of the United States of*

America, a comprehensive formulary for doctors and pharmacists first published in 1833, recommended olive oil as a treatment for a variety of conditions, including chronic constipation and gall bladder disease. Olive oil also appears to have been used to treat malnutrition. And in World War I, a combination of olive oil, malted milk powder, and hot water or milk was given to war-weary soldiers who suffered from nervous disorders.

So far, our historical overview has focused mainly on the olive and its oil, but as hinted at earlier, the olive leaf, too, has been used as a remedy for various ills. For hundreds of years, traditional practitioners have valued the leaf for its ability to lower fever, to heal wounds, to cure infection, to relieve skin rashes and boils, and to cleanse the liver. In the early 1800s, French soldiers used olive leaves to treat "intermittent fever." Later, in the mid-nineteenth century, an article in the *Pharmaceutical Journal of Provincial Transactions* reported that "a decoction of the leaves" of the olive tree was found to be effective in reducing fevers caused by a severe disease that had swept the island of Mytelene in 1843. Subsequently, the olive leaf was found to have greater fever-lowering properties than quinine.

Clearly, the products of the olive tree have been found to have amazing properties. How does the olive heal wounds, lower fever, and do so much more? Modern science has found some important answers in the laboratory.

WHAT'S IN THE OLIVE TREE?

As you learned in the brief history provided above, not just the olive itself but also the silvery leaves of the olive tree—and even its buds and bark—appear to have curative powers. In fact, the more we learn about this beautiful tree, the easier it is to understand why ancient cultures viewed it as a gift of the gods.

Like the olive and its oil, the leaf of the olive tree has long been known to possess healthful properties. Over the years, it has been used to lower fever, heal wounds, cure infection, and effectively treat a variety of other ills.

The Olive

Nutritionally speaking, 100 grams of cured green olives provide 116 calories, 12.7 grams of fat, 1.4 grams of protein, 1.3 grams of carbohydrates, and 61 milligrams of calcium. The same quantity of black (ripe) olives offers 129 calories, 13.8 grams of fat, 1.1 grams of protein, 2.6 grams of carbohydrates, and 94.1 milligrams of calcium. Delicious as they are, olives are clearly high in fat. But as most people know by now, the monounsaturated fat present in olives—and, of course, in olive oils—is *exactly* the kind of friendly fat your body requires. The inset on pages 54 to 55 provides a short refresher course on fats, highlighting the benefits of monounsaturates. For now, let it suffice to say that this is the fat that reduces the risk of heart disease by decreasing the buildup of fatty deposits in the arteries, and actually removing any existing arterial buildup.

Laboratory analysis has shown that the olive is packed with antioxidants— substances that provide powerful protection against a variety of disorders.

The beneficial substances in olives don't end with the fruit's monounsaturated fats, though. Olives also contain Vitamins A, D, E, and K. Of these, Vitamin E is present in largest amounts; 100 grams of olive oil contain about 19.4 milligrams of the vitamin. And all of these vitamins are antioxidants—substances thought to be effective in helping prevent cancer, heart disease, and other disorders. Olives also contain compounds called polyphenols, with 10 grams of extra virgin olive oil providing 5 milligrams of polyphenols. These compounds, which are found in plant-based foods, are also known to be powerful antioxidants.

The Olive Leaves and Bark

As discussed earlier in the chapter, the leaves of the olive tree have long been known to have health benefits, including the ability to heal wounds and fight infection. But only recently did scientists discover the substance responsible for many of the olive leaf's powers—oleuropein.

In Chapter 2, you learned that oleuropein is present in the fruit of the olive tree, but that this bitter-tasting substance is removed during the curing process. We now know that oleuropein is actually present throughout the olive tree—in the leaves, buds, wood, bark, and roots. In fact, this is the compound that is thought to make the tree particularly vigorous and resistant to insect and bacterial damage.

Oleuropein's antimicrobial activity occurs when it breaks down in the body, forming elolenic acid. Elolenic acid then interferes with the replication process of most pathogens, such as infection-causing bacteria, enabling the immune system to protect the body from disease. Oleuropein is thus regarded by many experts as having antibiotic, anti-bacterial, anti-viral, and anti-fungal properties. (You'll learn more about the healing power of olive leaves on page 60.)

Before we move on, it should be noted that oleuropein probably isn't the only compound responsible for the olive leaf's ability to heal and cure. This silvery leaf also seems to be packed with flavonoids such as rutin, apigenin, and luteolin. Water-soluble plant pigments, flavonoids are known to support good health by reducing inflammation, fighting viral infection, and protecting blood vessels.

Scientists believe that *oleuropein*, the same substance that makes fresh olives bitter, is also responsible for the olive leaf's anti-microbial properties—as well as the tree's legendary health and vigor.

HOW DOES THE OLIVE TREE AFFECT YOUR HEALTH?

You now know about some of the powerfully beneficial substances found in the olive tree. But have actual studies supported the benefits of this ancient plant? Let's see what science has to say about the relationship between olives and your health.

The Olive

The simple fact that olives are rich in monounsaturated fats and antioxi-

Getting the Skinny on Fats

In recent years, nearly everyone has learned at least one fact about olives and their oil: They promote health by providing a healthy dose of monounsaturated fats. To understand this statement, it's necessary to learn a few basics about the different fats found in our foods.

Saturated Fats

Saturated fats—so called because they are fully saturated with hydrogen atoms—are found in meats, poultry, and all dairy products that contain whole milk, such as cheese, butter, sour cream, and heavy cream. The tropical oils, which are made from coconut and palm kernels, are also high in saturated fat. You can usually tell that a fat is saturated because, if the proportion of this fat is high in a food, it is solid at room temperature. Butter, for instance, is full of saturated fats.

A heavy intake of saturated fat is associated with a higher risk of heart disease primarily because this fat raises blood cholesterol levels, and thus leads to clogged arteries.

Polyunsaturated Fats

Polyunsaturated fats are those fats found in leafy green plants; certain fish; nuts; seeds; and vegetable oils like sunflower, safflower, and corn oils—as well as the margarine, mayonnaise, and salad dressings made from these oils. When polyunsaturated vegetable oils arrived on the scene, they were touted as a healthier alternative to saturated fats. And, in fact, they do lower cholesterol levels. (You'll learn more about this later.) But in the last few years, it has been found that when eaten in excess, polyunsaturated vegetable oils also generate free radicals—substances known to damage cells and promote the development of blood clots, high blood pressure, and other disorders.

Should you avoid these oils entirely? No, because certain polyunsaturated fats are actually essential to life. However, it is important to limit the consumption of vegetable oils that are high in polyunsaturates.

Hydrogenated Fats

Before we turn this discussion to our hero, olive oil, we should briefly look at a substance that is becoming more and more common in our foods—hydrogenated fat. This is different from the other fats being discussed because it is artificially manufactured through the addition of hydrogen to liquid vegetable oils. This process transforms liquid oils into solid shortenings, giving them a butter-like consistency, improving their baking qualities, and extending their shelf life. That's why you'll find hydrogenated oils listed among the ingredients in cookies, crackers, and margarines.

Unfortunately, the hydrogenation process also creates by-products known as trans-fatty acids or trans fats. And trans fats have been found to act much like saturated fats, raising blood cholesterol levels. In fact, one study conducted by Harvard University estimated that each year, between 30,000 and 100,000 premature deaths from heart disease are caused by the effects of trans fats.

Monounsaturated Fats

Monounsaturated fats are found in avocados, almonds, cashews, peanuts, macadamia nuts, canola oil, and, of course, olive oil. While, as you now know, saturated fats, trans fats, and sometimes even polyunsaturated fats can cause a host of serious health problems, monounsaturated fats are not only safe to eat, but actually beneficial, primarily because of the way they affect the particles that transport cholesterol throughout the body.

Cholesterol circulates in the bloodstream in particles called lipoproteins. Low-density lipoproteins (LDLs), also known as "bad" cholesterol, trans-port cholesterol throughout the body to the cells that need them. If the LDLs are carrying more cholesterol than the cells can use, however, the excess is deposited in the form of artery-clogging plaque. Fortunately, there are also high-density lipoproteins (HDLs), known as "good" cholesterol. HDLs carry cholesterol away from the cells and back to the liver for recycling or disposal. Your balance of LDLs and HDLs, then, determines how much cholesterol will be deposited in your blood vessels.

What does this have to do with fats? Well, saturated fats raise cholesterol by raising the bad LDLs and lowering the good HDLs. This is clearly the worst possible scenario. A better but still imperfect scenario is provided by polyunsaturated fats, which lower cholesterol by lowering both the bad LDLs and good HDLs. Of course, the best scenario would be to lower the bad LDLs and raise the good HDLs. And which type of fat does that? Monounsaturated fats, of course. Moreover, no naturally produced oil has as large an amount of monounsaturated fats as olive oil. The modest amount of polyunsaturated fats in olive oil is well protected by the olive's antioxidants, providing a mechanism that delays aging and prevents carcinogenesis. All of this combines to make olive oil the perfect heart-healthy oil!

dants is a clue that this wonderful fruit is heart-healthy. Research has not only confirmed this, but has also shown that the olive—or, more specifically, its oil—benefits the body in many different ways, some of which are truly surprising.

Olive Oil and Cardiovascular Disease

In the mid-1900s, a young scientist named Ancel Keys noted a link between the olive oil-rich Mediterranean diet and cardiovascular health. Since then, numerous studies have shown that olive oil helps reduce cholesterol, thereby decreasing the risk of heart attack and other cardiovascular disorders.

Scientists first became aware of the relationship between olives and cardiovascular health more than fifty years ago, when they noted the effects of the Mediterranean diet. In Greece, southern Italy, southern France, and many other parts of the Mediterranean, the diet is very different from daily fare in other European countries and North America. Mediterranean cultures eat lots of fruit and vegetables, whole grains, and fish; only small amounts of meat; and relatively large amounts of fat, 90 percent of which comes from olive oil. While researchers expected the rate of heart disease to be high considering the high fat intake, it was not. In fact, it was found that people who follow a Mediterranean diet have far lower rates of heart attack and other cardiovascular disease than do those who follow standard American and European diets. Furthermore, the lowest rates of heart disease occur in Greece, where olive oil intake is highest.

The virtues of the Mediterranean diet have been promoted ever since. And in the last fifty years, numerous studies have proven that olive oil helps reduce levels of total and LDL cholesterol ("bad" cholesterol), thereby reducing the risk of cardiovascular disease.

In seeking to understand the association between cardiovascular health and olive oil consumption, some researchers questioned if olive oil reduces the blood's clotting ability, which would in turn mean fewer heart attacks. Indeed, studies show that levels of blood coagulation factor VII are significantly lower in those who include olive oil in their diets.

Researchers have also found a strong correlation between olive oil consumption and low blood pressure. For many years, they had known that the characteristics of a Mediterranean diet—with its high fruit and vegetable intake and high proportion of monounsaturated fats—are important in controlling blood pressure levels. To further investigate this link, they designed a study to examine the effects of a diet high in monounsaturates versus a diet high in polyunsaturates. For six months, twenty-three people with mild to moderate hypertension (high blood pressure) were randomly assigned to either a diet high in virgin olive oil or a diet high in sunflower oil. Then the groups switched diets. Researchers found that while consuming the extra virgin olive oil diet, subjects reduced the amount of medication necessary to control blood pressure levels by 48 percent, while the sunflower oil group had only a 4-percent reduction of medication. Moreover, eight subjects on the olive oil diet required no antihypertensive drugs at all, while all subjects on the sunflower oil diet had to remain on medication. It was concluded that a diet high in monounsaturated fats and low in other fats can reduce blood pressure levels and either reduce or eliminate the need for antihypertensive drugs.

Researchers and nutritionists emphasize that olive oil is no panacea. Rather, they stress that it helps protect the heart only if it is part of a healthy diet—a diet high in fruits, vegetables, and whole grains, and low in animal fats.

Olive Oil and Cancer

As researchers investigated cultures that follow a Mediterranean diet, they found that not just rates of cardiovascular disease but also rates of cancer are relatively low. Studies have borne out the link between olive oil and a reduced risk of cancer.

Although olive oil has been found to promote cardiovascular health in a number of ways, researchers emphasize that the oil is heart-healthy only when part of a diet rich in fruits, vegetables, and whole grains.

To learn more about the relationship of diet and cancer, a team of medical researchers in Barcelona, Spain carried out a study on rats. The animals were broken into three groups, with one group receiving a diet rich in olive oil; another group, a diet rich in fish oil; and another, a diet rich in safflower oil. Half of each of these groups was then given a cancer-causing agent. Four months later, the researchers found that those rats on the olive oil diet had less precancerous tissue and fewer tumors than those fed the other oils. Scientists believe that the antioxidant constituents in olive oil may help to protect against cancer.

Population studies have led to similar conclusions. A team of researchers at the Institute of Health Sciences compared colon cancer rates, diet, and olive oil consumption in twenty-eight countries, including Europe, Britain, the United States, Brazil, Colombia, Canada, and China. They found that countries with a diet high in meat and low in vegetables had the highest rates of colon cancer, but that olive oil was associated with a decreased risk. Researchers think that olive oil reduces the amount of bile acid and increases levels of the enzyme thought to beneficially regulate cell turnover in the gut.

Studies have also linked the consumption of olive oil with a reduced risk of breast cancer. The *Archives of Internal Medicine* reported the findings of researchers who studied the diets of more than 60,000 women between the ages of 40 and 76. After a period of three years, scientists found that those subjects who did not develop breast cancer had a higher intake of olive oil. The research further suggested that a spoonful of olive oil a day can reduce the risk of developing breast cancer by as much as 45 percent.

Like the scientists who study cardiovascular health, cancer researchers stress the importance of a healthy diet, rather than the addition of olive oil to a diet that is otherwise poor. Scientists at the Institute of Health Sciences, for instance, found that many factors affect the rate of colon cancer. They

Both laboratory and population studies indicate that diets high in olive oil help reduce the risk of colon cancer and breast cancer.

concluded that a cancer-protective diet should be low in meat and fish in addition to being rich in olive oil.

Olive Oil and Osteoporosis

The association between olive oil consumption and good health has spurred a number of studies. Perhaps surprisingly, one of them focused on the incidence of osteoporosis, a disease that can lead to weak and brittle bones.

The study, conducted by the University of Athens, involved 118 women and 32 men of ages 25 to 69. Researchers found that the more olive oil the subjects consumed, the denser their bones and the greater their bone mass, resulting in a lesser tendency towards osteoporosis and fractures. One of the most encouraging discoveries was that olive oil appears to have beneficial effects even after the age of 40. This is good news, as many experts feel that calcium provides a defense against bone loss only if it is consumed in the first twenty years of life and accompanied by exercise. The *British Medical Journal* stated that the Greek study—the first to link bone health with olive oil consumption—was highly significant.

Researchers believe that some of the bone-protective properties of olive oil can be attributed to its Vitamin E content. They emphasize, though, that the oil contains 200 elements, many of which are only now being studied.

Surprisingly, olive oil-rich diets appear to strengthen bones, reducing the risk of osteoporosis. Better yet, unlike calcium, olive oil is believed to support bone health even when consumed later in life.

Olive Oil and Weight Loss

Tablespoon for tablespoon, all fats—from olive oil to corn oil to butter—are high in calories. The logical conclusion is that if consumed in excess, olive oil, like any other fat, will contribute to weight gain.

One study, however, has raised questions about this assumption. Researchers at Brigham and Women's Hospital in Boston examined two groups. Each of the groups followed a 1,200 calories-a-day diet, but while one group limited fat intake to 20 percent of calories, the other followed a Mediterranean-style diet that drew 35-percent of its calories from the fats found in olive oil, nuts, and other natural foods. While both groups initially lost weight, after eighteen months, the low-fat group had begun to regain lost pounds, while the Mediterranean-style group had maintained its weight loss. Members of the second group reported that their diet plan was easy to follow because it permitted them to use full-fat salad dressings and other satisfying foods, and therefore kept them from feeling hungry and deprived.

Like other researchers, those involved in the Brigham and Women's Hospital study do not advocate a high-fat diet. They do, however, feel that when olive oil and other wholesome foods are part of a well-balanced, calorie-controlled eating plan, the result is greater well-being, including healthy body weight.

The Olive Leaf

Earlier in the chapter, you learned that the substance thought to be responsible for the olive leaf's healing powers is oleuropein, a compound that appears to be present throughout the tree. For the most part, it is this substance—as well as elolenic acid, which is formed in the body when oleuropein is metabolized—that has been used in the growing research on the olive leaf.

The Olive Leaf and Infection

You already know that traditional practitioners have long used the olive leaf to fight infection and disease. In the twentieth century, scientific research confirmed the potency of this natural substance.

In the 1960s, research at the Upjohn Company, a major American pharmaceutical firm, found conclusive evidence that elolenic acid inhibits the growth of viruses. In fact, researchers discovered that olive leaf extracts were effective in test tube experiments against the herpes virus, many influenza and parainfluenza viruses, and a host of other viruses, as well as certain bacteria and parasitic protozoans. Those who worked on the studies attributed the broad killing power of the olive leaf to a number of the leaf's unique properties, including an ability to interfere with critical amino acid production essential for the existence of the virus; an ability to contain viral infection and/or spread by inactivating the virus; and an ability to directly penetrate infected cells and stop viral replication. Thus, the active compound found in the leaf appears to offer healing effects not provided by pharmaceutical antibiotics and other products.

Apparently, Upjohn abandoned its research into the olive leaf derivative because the company was unable to produce a synthetic version that worked as effectively as the natural extract, and thus was unable to patent it. However, many fine natural olive extracts are now available in health food stores, offering the power of the leaf in a variety of products.

Research has shown that olive leaf extract has the ability to resist or overcome a remarkably wide range of infectious organisms, from bacteria to viruses to parasitic protozoans.

The Olive Leaf and Cardiovascular Disease

Interestingly, it was an Italian scientist's findings about olive leaf extract that initially triggered the flurry of scientific interest in the leaf. The researcher reported that oleuropein significantly lowered blood pressure in animals—and subsequent investigations by European researchers confirmed this finding. At Spain's University of Granada, for instance, pharmacologists determined that olive leaf extract causes relaxation of arterial walls in laboratory animals, which, in turn, can help relieve hypertension. Moreover, European studies have shown that oleuropein can normalize arrhythmias (irregularities in heartbeat).

Other studies have suggested additional ways in which the olive leaf may improve cardiovascular function. Researchers at the University of Milan's Institute of Pharmacological Studies, for instance, found that oleuropein inhibits the oxidation of low-density lipoproteins (LDLs), the so-called "bad" cholesterol discussed in the inset on page 55. This means that oleuropein helps prevent the action through which LDLs promote the

The Naturally Healing Olive

In days gone by, herbalists and natural healers used olive oil, olive leaves, and even the bark of the olive tree to treat a number of ills, from aches and pains to fever and congestion. The following "recipes" will allow you to make natural remedies rich in the healing power of the olive. Just remember that in the case of any serious condition such as hypertension—or any condition that persists for more than a few days—you should consult a physician.

OLIVE LEAF TEA

2 teaspoons crushed olive leaves

5 ounces boiling water

The next time you're suffering from a cold or the flu, use this tea for its antiviral properties. Olive Leaf Tea can also help fight chronic fatigue.

1. Place the crushed olive leaves in a cup, and pour the water over the leaves. Allow to steep for 30 minutes.

2. Pour the tea through a strainer, and discard the leaves. Drink 3 to 4 times a day.

COLD AND COUGH COMPRESS

This folk cure has been relied on for centuries.
Use it overnight to relieve congestion and coughs.

$^1/_2$ cup olive oil

$^1/_2$ cup camphor
(available in most
pharmacies)

$^1/_2$ cup vinegar

1. Place all of the ingredients in a medium-sized bowl, and stir to combine.

2. To use, soak a piece of clean woolen cloth in the mixture and wring out gently, leaving the cloth thoroughly saturated. Apply the compress to the chest, overwrapping with a dry piece of wool to keep the compress in place. Leave on overnight.

SINUS MASK

Folk healers say that this old-time mask works fast
to open clogged sinuses and restore easy breathing.

2 tablespoons
olive oil

I teaspoon
dry mustard

1. Place the olive oil and dry mustard in a small bowl, and stir to combine.

2. To use, smooth the mixture over your forehead, paying particular attention to the area above your eyebrows. Avoid getting any of the mask in your eyes. Massage the mask in firmly. Then lie down for 10 minutes, elevating your feet above your head. Rinse the mask off with warm water.

OLIVE OIL AND ST. JOHN'S WORT LINIMENT

2–4 flowering stalks
of St. John's wort

¾ cup hot water

2 cups olive oil

Combining healing St. John's wort
with soothing olive oil, this liniment
is great for arthritis pain and sore muscles.

1. Strip the flowers from the stalk, and place them in a medium-sized bowl. Using the back of a spoon, crush the flowers against the bowl.

2. Add the hot water to the bowl, and encourage the flowers to stay beneath the water. Allow the mixture to cool.

3. Blend the olive oil into the cooled mixture. Then pour the mixture into a wide-mouthed jar large enough to allow the mixture to double in volume. Do not cover.

4. Place the jar in a warm place for 3 to 5 days, stirring daily. Bubbles will form as the mixture ferments.

5. Cap the jar tightly, and store in a dark place for about 6 weeks, or until the oil has turned a luminous red. (The red color comes from the small dark points on the petals and inside the calyx.)

6. Carefully pour off the oil that has risen to the top, and store in a glass bottle with an airtight lid. (Discard the watery layer of flowers.) To use, rub the oil onto the affected area as often as needed.

development of arterial plaque, the substance that narrows and blocks the arteries. On the basis of these findings, the scientists hypothesized that olive leaf extract may possess powerful antioxidant properties, and so may provide the body with protection against a number of other disorders, as well.

Clinically, olive leaf extract has been used for a relatively short period of time. Initial results seem positive, however, and further research seems certain to provide a greater understanding of the olive leaf's healthful components.

OLIVE OIL AND BEAUTY

So far, this chapter has focused on what olive oil can do for you on the inside. But olive oil benefits the outside, as well. The oil of the olive has long been called the "beauty oil," as its valuable fatty acids, as well as its bounty of vitamins, make skin and hair lustrous—and not only when taken internally. The ancient Greeks rubbed olive oil into their skin to soften and moisten it, and rubbed it into their scalp and hair to maintain health and shine. From ancient times, women have encouraged the growth of luxuriant eyelashes by brushing them with olive oil. And a time-honored method of treating ragged cuticles and brittle fingernails is to massage olive oil into the area nightly.

Upon reaching 101 years of age, Frenchwoman Jeanne Calmont was asked the secret of her beauty and longevity. Her reply was that she ate olives and enjoyed olive oil on her vegetables and salads every day, as well as rubbing olive oil into her skin daily. As proof that the treatment works, she added triumphantly, "I have only one wrinkle—and I'm sitting on it!" Calmont was listed in the *Guinness Book of World Records* as the world's oldest living person when she died in 1997 at the age of 122.

Following in the footsteps of generations of beautiful women, many

Since the time of the ancient Greeks, olive oil—both as a food and as a component in cosmetics—has been used to enhance the beauty of skin, hair, and nails.

cosmetics companies now incorporate olive oil and olive oil extracts into their cleansers, moisturizers, body scrubs, hair conditioners, and a host of other products. But you don't have to buy an expensive commercial cream or conditioner to benefit from the oil of the olive. The remainder of this chapter offers a selection of recipes for tried-and-true products that you can whip up in your own home.

OLIVE AND OATS MOISTURIZING LOTION

2 teaspoons oatmeal, pounded or processed in a blender until fine

1–2 teaspoons olive oil

$\frac{1}{2}$ cup very hot water

Oats are an ancient grain that, like olives, originated in the Mediterranean region. Perhaps that's why these two natural products go together so well. Use this easy-to-make lotion to give your skin a soothing dose of moisture.

1. Place the oatmeal and olive oil in a small bowl, and stir to form a paste.

2. Drizzle the hot water into the oatmeal paste, stirring as you do to combine thoroughly.

3. Allow the mixture to cool. Then pour it through muslin or a double layer of cheesecloth into a small bowl. Squeeze the cloth to extract all the liquid. Then discard the cloth and its contents.

4. To use, gently massage the liquid onto your face, paying particular attention to any dry areas that need softening. Also apply to rough spots on elbows, knees, and heels. Allow the mixture to soak in for at least 30 minutes. Rinse off with lukewarm water.

5. Apply 2 or 3 times a day, as needed. Make the mixture fresh each day.

OLIVE OIL AND CREAM FACE CLEANSER

This super-rich cleanser is perfect for dry skin.
Use it as often as you like without fear of causing dryness or flaking.

1. Grate the soap coarsely, or sliver it with a sharp knife.

2. Place the soap in the top of a double boiler. Stir the ¾ cup of water into the soap, cover, and cook over simmering water, stirring occasionally, until the soap has melted. When well blended, remove from the heat.

3. Combine the cream and olive oil in a small saucepan. Place over low heat and cook, stirring constantly, until blended. Do not allow the mixture to boil.

4. When the olive oil mixture is hot, stir it into the soap and water mixture. Whisk together until the two solutions are well blended.

5. Add the benzoic acid powder to the soap mixture, and whisk to combine until the powder is thoroughly incorporated.

6. Pour the cleanser into a wide-mouthed bottle with a lid, and store in a cool place. Do not refrigerate.

7. To use, massage the cleanser into your skin with your fingertips. Rinse off with lukewarm water.

I small cake mild glycerine soap

¾ cup water

¼ cup heavy cream

2 teaspoons olive oil

2 pinches benzoic acid powder (available in most pharmacies)

OLIVE OIL AND STRAWBERRY FACE CLEANSER

8–10 fresh
strawberries

2 teaspoons sweet
almond oil (available
in most health food
stores)

$\frac{1}{2}$ cup olive oil

*Made with both nourishing oil and refreshing strawberry juice,
this is the perfect cleanser for normal skin—
skin that is neither oily nor excessively dry.*

1. Wash and dry the strawberries. Grate the strawberries or rub them against a wire strainer, catching the juice in a measuring cup. When you have 1 ounce, or 2 tablespoons, discard the pulp that has accumulated in the strainer.

2. Blend the almond oil into the strawberry juice. Slowly add the olive oil, whisking continually until well incorporated. Pour the cleanser into a wide-mouthed bottle with a lid, and store in a cool place, but do not refrigerate. The oils will separate while standing, so shake well before using.

3. To use, massage the cleanser into your skin with your fingertips, avoiding the area around the eyes. Expect a tingle from the acid in the strawberry juice. Rinse off with lukewarm water, and finish with a splash of cool water to close your pores.

OLIVE OIL AND LEMON CREAM FACE CLEANSER

*Designed for oily skin, this cleanser
will remove both makeup and excess oil.*

1. Grate or sliver the wax.

2. Place the wax in the top of a double boiler. Stir in the petroleum jelly, olive oil, and lanolin, and cook over simmering water, stirring occasionally, until the wax and lanolin liquefy and are well blended with the petroleum jelly and olive oil. Turn off the heat, but keep the pan over the hot water.

3. Combine the water, lemon juice, and benzoic acid powder in a small saucepan. Place over very low heat and bring to a bare simmer, stirring constantly.

4. Drizzle the hot lemon juice mixture into the hot wax mixture, stirring continually. Beat vigorously until the mixture begins to cool. Then beat in the oil of lemon.

5. Pour the cleanser into a wide-mouthed jar with a lid.

6. To use, first steam your pores open by soaking a washcloth in hot water, wringing it out, and applying it to your face. Repeat several times. Then, avoiding the area around your eyes, smooth the cleanser over your face, concentrating on any particularly oily spots. Wait at least 2 minutes before removing with a tissue. Finish with a hot water steam to remove every trace of oil, and close your pores with a splash of cool water.

$1/2$ ounce white beeswax (available in most health food stores)

2 tablespoons Vaseline petroleum jelly

2 tablespoons olive oil

1 tablespoon waterless lanolin (available in most pharmacies)

$1 1/2$ tablespoons distilled water

1 tablespoon fresh lemon juice, strained

2 pinches benzoic acid powder (available in most pharmacies)

2 drops oil of lemon

OLIVE OIL AND EGG DEEP-CLEANING MASK

I egg, separated

2 tablespoons
olive oil

½ teaspoon alcohol

*Use this mask to deep-clean your pores
and remove any makeup residue or grime.*

1. Place the egg yolk in a small bowl. Using a fork, blend the oil into the yolk. Then mix in the alcohol.

2. Whisk the egg white until frothy. Fold the beaten egg white into the oil mixture.

3. To use, first steam your pores open by soaking a washcloth in hot water, wringing it out, and applying it to your face. Repeat several times. Then, avoiding the area around your eyes, smooth the mask over your face. If you have a clean, soft brush, use it to apply the mask.

4. Leave the mask in place for 20 to 30 minutes. If possible, lie down while the mask is working. Then rinse the mask off with lukewarm water. Finish with a splash of cool water to close your pores.

OLIVE OIL AND APPLE TONING MASK

I apple

2 tablespoons
olive oil

*Use this mask to freshen
and tone tired skin.*

1. Peel, core, and grate the apple coarsely. Stir in the olive oil.

2. To use, first steam your pores open by soaking a washcloth in hot water, wringing it out, and applying it to your face. Repeat several times. Then, avoiding the area around your eyes, smooth the mask over your face.

3. Leave the mask in place for 20 to 30 minutes. If possible, lie down while the mask is working. Then rinse the mask off with lukewarm water. Finish with a splash of cool water to close your pores.

OLIVE OIL AND HONEY SOFTENING MASK

This rich mask softens, smoothes, and nourishes.
Use it not just on your face, but on any area of your body
that would benefit from a dose of moisture.

1 tablespoon
olive oil

1 tablespoon honey

2 teaspoons
cornstarch

1. Place the olive oil and honey in a small bowl, and whisk together until well blended.

2. Slowly sprinkle the cornstarch into the mixture while stirring. Add just enough to make a smooth paste that doesn't run.

3. To use, first steam your pores open by soaking a washcloth in hot water, wringing it out, and applying it to your face. Repeat several times. Then, avoiding the area around your eyes, smooth the mask over your face.

4. Leave the mask in place for 20 to 30 minutes. If possible, lie down while the mask is working. Then rinse the mask off with lukewarm water. Finish with a splash of cool water to close your pores.

OLIVE OIL AND EGG TIGHTENING MASK

2 eggs, separated

¹/₂ cup olive oil

*The olive in this mask nourishes the skin, while the
egg firms and tightens. Use it before applying makeup,
and you'll be ready for a night out on the town.*

1. Place the egg yolks in a small bowl, and whisk the olive oil into the yolks.

2. To use, first steam your pores open by soaking a washcloth in hot water, wringing it out, and applying it to your face. Repeat several times. Then, avoiding the area around your eyes, smooth the yolk mixture over your face. Leave in place for 10 minutes.

3. Beat the egg whites until stiff. Apply over the egg yolk mixture. Then lie down with your feet higher than your head and relax for 30 minutes.

4. Rinse the mask off with lukewarm water and a washcloth. Finish with a splash of cool water to close your pores.

OLIVE OIL AND HONEY HAIR CONDITIONER

¹/₂ cup honey

3 tablespoons olive oil

Use this conditioner to make your hair lustrous and manageable.

1. Place the honey and olive oil in a small bowl, and stir well to mix.

2. To use, work the conditioner through freshly washed, towel-dried hair. Then wrap your hair in plastic wrap and leave the conditioner in the hair for 10 minutes. If desired, to help the conditioner penetrate the hair, wrap a towel still warm from the dryer over the plastic wrap. Rinse well with warm water and style as usual.

OLIVE OIL AND TEA EYE SOOTHER

This simple treatment will soothe the eye area, reducing puffiness.

1 cup boiling water

2 tea bags

½ teaspoon olive oil

1. Place the boiling water in a cup, and add the tea bags. Allow them to steep for 2 minutes. Then squeeze the excess water from the bags and allow them to cool until comfortable to the touch.

2. Place the olive oil in a small saucepan, and heat until slightly warm but still comfortable to the touch. Do not allow the oil to get hot.

3. To use, gently pat the oil around your eyes and on your eyelids. Then lie down with your feet elevated and place the tea bags over your eyes, pressing gently to shape them to the eye area. Allow them to remain in place for 10 minutes.

4. Remove the tea bags, and pat the area with a clean tissue to remove the excess oil.

EGG AND OLIVE OIL HAIR CONDITIONER

Use this super-rich conditioner to repair your hair when shampooing, blow-drying, sun, or wind have left it dry and damaged.

2 eggs

¼ cup olive oil

1. Place the eggs in a small bowl, and stir in the olive oil.

2. To use, work the conditioner through freshly washed, towel-dried hair. Then wrap your hair in plastic wrap and leave the conditioner in the hair for 10 minutes. If desired, to help the conditioner penetrate the hair, wrap a towel still warm from the dryer over the plastic wrap. Rinse well with warm water and style as usual.

If you previously thought of the olive tree only as a source of savory snacks and golden oil, this chapter has, hopefully, opened your eyes to the healing and beautifying powers of the olive tree. In fact, you may now be so impressed by the sophisticated and versatile olive that you want a tree (or two) all your own. If so, you're in luck. The next chapter will guide you in growing the beautiful olive tree in your own backyard.

CHAPTER 5

Olives in Your Own Backyard

These trees so fresh, so full, so beautiful;
when they display their fruit, green, golden, and black . . .
it is among the most agreeable sights one might ever see.

—MIGUEL DE CERVANTES SAAVEDRA (1547–1616)

I f you've read the earlier chapters of this book, there's a good chance that you've fallen in love with the olive tree. With its fabulously twisted trunk, its silvery foliage, and its creamy white flowers, the olive tree is truly a thing of beauty—in addition, of course, to being a source of the wonderfully versatile olive fruit. Fortunately, in most areas, the splendor of the olive tree can be yours to enjoy right in your own backyard. Depending on the climate in your region, you may have to make certain adjustments; you may, for instance, have to choose one variety of olives over another, or grow your tree in a container instead of your garden. But by following some basic guidelines, you'll be able to select a tree, plant it, care for it, and—if you're lucky—even harvest its luscious fruit. This chapter will show you how it's done.

UNDERSTANDING THE EFFECT OF CLIMATE

When preparing to grow an olive tree in your own backyard, there are many factors over which you *can* exercise control. You can, for instance, modify soil composition through the use of specific fertilizers, or choose a sunny site over a shady one. Unfortunately, though, you cannot control climate. But by understanding the effect of climate on the olive tree, you will know what to expect from your tree, and will be able to make any adjustments necessitated by your region.

As you learned in Chapter 2, *Olea europaea* is a native of the Mediterranean, and loves a hot climate. A long, hot growing season is needed to properly ripen the fruit. However, studies have shown that the tree won't bear fruit unless it's been exposed to chilly temperatures during the winter. When winters are warm, the tree does not realize that it's winter, and keeps growing. Then when spring comes, the tree does not realize that it's time to produce flowers—nor does it have the reserve nutrients available to do so. No flowers equals no fruit. Worldwide, the magic numbers for good fruit set are clear, sunny days over 70°F degrees, and a temperature range of 45°F to 50°F at night during the winter months.

While *Olea europaea* likes cool winter nights, it cannot endure sustained periods of extreme cold. If your area experiences cold winters but temperatures remain above 17°F, you can cultivate your olive tree as an ornamental. In other words, your tree will grow, but will not bear fruit. If temperatures in your region dip below 17°F, your tree may sustain damage to leaves and small stems; if they fall below 12°F, the damage is likely to be

Olive trees are most likely to thrive and produce bounteous harvests when summers are long and hot, and winters provide the chill needed to set fruit.

more severe; and if they fall below 10°F, the tree will probably not survive at all if left out-of-doors. However, even in areas with such severe winters, your olive tree can be grown in a container that permits you to place the plant outside during the warmer months, and move it indoors before the winter can do any harm.

Before we end our discussion of climate, let's briefly turn our attention to rainfall. Due to the olive tree's hardiness and adaptability, the majority of varietals can survive in just about any climate, and withstand even severe drought. However, olives grow best in areas with winter-dominant rainfall that ranges from twenty to thirty-two inches. In many regions, therefore, irrigation is needed to promote fruiting.

If you are interested in growing olive trees for fruit and you're not sure about your region's suitability, try contacting the National Weather Service, which can provide you with climatic data for your general region. Be aware, though, that this general information may not be correct for your specific property. Different areas have been known to vary significantly even within a single weather map region.

Although the hardy olive tree can survive even severe drought, sufficient water is needed if the tree is to bear fruit. When an area's rainfall is inadequate, growers usually use irrigation to insure good fruiting from year to year.

CHOOSING A SITE

In general, olives are not fussy. They are suited to almost any soil condition, including rocky terrain. However, the olive tree does need good drainage. Olives aren't happy living in swamp-like conditions with wet, heavy soil. Therefore, it is essential to avoid areas that collect water, seep water after rain, or hold moisture in to the point of becoming soggy. Be aware that some soils won't drain sufficiently no matter what steps are taken to improve the situation. Also keep in mind that a sloping site does not necessarily insure good drainage. When heavy clay soils are on steep sites, for example, they generally are not suitable for the cultivation of olive

Although the olive tree is not picky about the soil in which it grows, it does demand good drainage. For best results when planting a tree, choose a site with sandy loam, loam, or clay loam.

Although beautiful, an olive tree can be messy. To avoid stains from falling fruit, plant your tree away from sidewalks, patios, and other surfaces that could be discolored.

trees because of poor internal drainage. The most advantageous soil types for olive trees are sandy loams, loams, and clay loams, as they usually have not only suitable drainage, but also adequate water-holding and nutrient-storage capacities.

Another consideration is the mineral content of the soil. Although the olive tree itself can survive a wide range of soil types, it will best produce fruit when the earth is rich in nitrogen, boron, and potassium, all of which support vigorous growth and high yields. Nitrogen has been shown to help increase fruit set; boron helps insure that your olives will remain on the tree until maturity; and potassium is needed for the new growth of fruiting wood and for good-sized fruit. In addition, for best results, the soil should have an alkaline pH of 7 to 8.

The only way to be certain of the composition and pH of your soil is to test it. Almost all garden centers sell test kits that analyze the level of certain minerals, as well as pH test kits that tell you whether your soil is acid or alkaline. Some nurseries will even test your soil free of charge. If a fertilizer seems indicated, a soil profile will tell you what your tree needs. Soil pH can be adjusted through the addition of lime.

Once you've considered your site's soil conditions, you'll want to look at its size. Olive trees like a lot of room. Although the roots of the tree are shallow, they reach out in spidery tentacles. Competition from trees growing within twenty feet of each other will not only slow growth, but also prevent the trees from bearing well. That's why experts agree that the proper space needed to allow young olive trees to grow is forty feet by forty feet.

Yet another concern is the amount of sun enjoyed by your tree's potential site. If possible, plant your olive tree in full sun, where it is sure to thrive. In addition, if your property permits, situate your tree away from sidewalks and other surfaces that could be stained from falling fruit. Or, as an alternative—and only if you are growing the tree as an ornamental—choose a nonfruiting olive variety.

If the location you've chosen is exposed to strong winds, don't worry. The winds will eventually "sculpt" the tree, but won't harm it. Olive trees are known for their wind-tolerance.

CHOOSING THE BEST TIME TO PLANT YOUR TREE

Because olive trees can be damaged by severe cold and physically stressed by excessive heat, and because young trees are particularly sensitive to extremes of temperature, it is clearly necessary to plant your tree when temperatures are moderate. In both California and the Mediterranean, many growers subscribe to the "warm soil, cool air philosophy," preferring to plant their trees in early fall. At that time, the intense heat of summer has passed, yet the soil is still relatively warm, and thus able to stimulate root growth. In most areas, planting in early autumn provides the tree with two months to harden before it's exposed to winter cold.

If your region experiences cold autumns, or if for any other reason you choose to plant at another time of year, early spring is another excellent choice. This allows the tree to avoid the frosts of December and January, as well as the extremes of summer heat, until it is well established.

To follow the "warm soil, cool air" rule, plant your tree in early fall, when your young olive plant will benefit from the warmth of the soil, and will not be stressed by severe summer heat.

CHOOSING THE BEST VARIETY

You've taken stock of your area's climate, chosen a site that offers good soil and sun conditions, and even selected the best time of year for planting. But what exactly are you going to plant? There are over 900 olive tree varieties, giving you a wide range of choices. Commercial growers, of course, employ specific criteria when choosing varieties, including the final product desired (table olives or oil), climate, and disease resistance. Their ultimate goal, of course, is to enjoy the highest possible yields and financial returns. Most likely, you are not growing your tree with the idea of starting a business, but you simply desire a plant that is healthy and beautiful and, perhaps, will provide you with your own private crop of fruit. Even so, you'll enjoy the greatest success if you choose a variety that is suited to your area.

Research conducted in California, the major olive-growing area of the United States, as well as in international olive-growing regions, has highlighted a number of varieties that thrive in certain temperature ranges. Of course, these are not the only cultivars that are suited to each of these climates, and your nursery may be able to suggest other plants that will do well in your area. But by basing your choice on the varieties suggested for each of the three following climates, you can help insure that the plant you choose will flourish in your backyard.

Although all olive trees are tolerant of most growing conditions, different varieties do thrive best in different temperature ranges. To help insure success, choose a tree that's suited to your area's climate.

Cold Climates

Cold olive-growing climates are defined as areas in which temperatures can fall below 18°F and snow may occasionally fall. Most of these regions grow only oil olives because these varieties are less prone to frost damage. It should be noted that although olive trees tend to sustain damage when temperatures fall below 17°F, as long as the low temperature does not continue for several hours, cold-climate olive trees remain unharmed. These olives also are able to withstand high summer temperatures and even a lack of ground moisture.

Varieties that grow and produce well in cold climates include Arbequina, Barouni, Coratina, Frantoio, Leccino, Maurino, Pendolino, and Sevillano.

Moderate Climates

Areas in which the lowest winter temperatures are generally 25°F to 27°F, and rarely dip below 21°F, are considered moderate olive-growing climates. Moderate climates, which provide the necessary chill for dormancy without damaging crops, are typical of the world's olive-growing regions.

Most of the varieties available for sale in North America grow well in moderate climates. These varieties include Arbequina, Barnea, Barouni, Frantoio, Hojiblanca, Kalamata, Leccino, Manzanillo, Moraiolo, Nevadillo Blanco, Picual, and Sevillano (Queen of Spain).

Warm Climates

Warm olive-growing climates have an average daily temperature of 54°F or less in January, but rarely experience frost or temperatures that fall below 28°F. This is the warmest climate considered suitable for olive production, as warmer conditions reduce the tree's ability to flower and fruit.

The varieties that are believed to be most successful in warm climates include Arbequina, Barouni, Frantoio, Kalamata, Manzanillo, and Nevadillo Blanco.

CHOOSING THE BEST PLANT

As discussed in Chapter 2, olive trees cannot be grown from seed, as the resulting plants will revert to the small-tree wild variety. As a result, commercially, olive trees are generally propagated by other means, such as cuttings. However, as a home grower who probably wants to plant only a tree or two, your best bet is to start with a young, well-established tree that's been grown by a reputable nursery. These trees come in one of three forms: container-grown trees; balled-and-burlapped (B&B) plants, which are

Even though every olive has a single pit that encloses one or two seeds, you cannot grow your tree from seed. Instead, purchase a young olive plant from a reputable nursery.

grown in nursery rows, after which their root balls are wrapped in either natural or plastic burlap; and bare-root plants, which are grown in the field, harvested, and then washed of all soil.

Of the three types of nursery plants, the container-grown and bur-lapped plants are the easiest to handle. However, bare-root plants do have certain advantages. First, they typically cost only 40 to 70 percent as much as container-grown plants. Second, they tend to become established more quickly and initially grow better than other plants. This is because when you plant a containerized or balled-and-burlapped plant, you put two soils—the soil surrounding the plant's roots and the soil at the planting site—in contact with each other, making it difficult for water to uniformly penetrate the rooting area. However, when you plant a bare-root olive tree, you refill the hole with soil dug from the hole, so the plant's roots grow in just one kind of soil, allowing the water to penetrate more evenly.

Whichever type of plant you choose to buy, make sure it is healthy before completing your purchase. Avoid plants that appear wilted or have off-color foliage, as these are signs that care has been poor or that the root system may have a problem. Leaves should be pliable yet firm, and full-sized. Branches should be well spaced.

When visiting a nursery, take care to choose a healthy olive tree for your backyard. Look for leaves that are pliable but firm; branches that are well spaced; and roots that are strong, fresh looking, and well formed.

In addition to checking the top of the tree, be sure to examine the root system. When choosing a bare-root olive tree, look for one with strong stems and fresh-looking, well-formed root systems. Avoid any plants with roots that are slimy or dry and withered. When buying a containerized tree, grasp the trunk of the tree near the base and try to move the tree in the container. The container and tree should move as one. Whether your tree is a B&B plant or containerized, ask a nursery employee for assistance in examining the roots. Healthy roots are firm and usually lighter in color than the surrounding soil. Be sure to check the odor of the roots, as well, and avoid any that have an offensive smell.

If you purchase a bare-root tree, be aware that it should be planted as soon as possible. If, however, you must wait because of bad weather, heel in the plant by laying it in a temporary trench dug in a shady spot. Cut off any extra-long roots, as well as any that are broken or otherwise damaged. Then cover the roots and a little of the trunk with soil, and water lightly. Keep the roots moist, but not soaking wet, until you're ready to introduce the young tree to its permanent home.

If your local nursery doesn't carry baby olive trees or doesn't offer the variety in which you're interested, it may be possible to have the nursery special-order one or two of the desired variety. Another option is to order your tree by mail from a reputable nursery. (See the Resource List on page 185.)

If you buy a bare-root tree and are unable to plant it right away, protect your purchase by laying it in a temporary trench and covering the roots with soil. Then keep the roots moist until you're ready to plant the tree either in your yard or in a container.

PLANTING YOUR OLIVE TREE

Hopefully, you have chosen a healthy olive tree that will delight you for many years to come. These glorious long-lived plants flourish and grow for centuries, providing beauty for generation after generation.

As you've learned, in areas like California, where winters are relatively warm, olive trees can thrive out-of-doors all year long. But in regions with harsh winters, these natives of the Mediterranean should be moved inside whenever temperatures threaten to drop below freezing. The following instructions will guide you through planting your young tree either out-doors or in a portable container.

Planting Your Tree Outdoors

If you've purchased an olive tree that that is container-grown or balled-and-burlapped, you will, of course, need to dig a hole that will accommo-date the root ball. Unlike many plants, the olive tree doesn't need a hole

A common mistake is to plant trees too deeply in the soil—a practice that deprives the roots of oxygen and makes the tree vulnerable to decay. To keep your olive tree healthy, be sure that the juncture between its roots and trunk is planted at or slightly above ground level.

that is two or three times the size of the roots. Instead, the hole should be just large enough to encase the roots and the dirt that surrounds them. If working with a containerized tree, plant the tree at the same depth at which it was planted in the pot. If *any* tree—not just an olive tree—is planted too deeply, or if it is placed on backfill that later settles and causes the plant to sink into the earth, the roots will be deprived of sufficient oxygen, causing the plant to decline and possibly die. An overly deep planting can also subject a tree to decay and damage. Remember that the juncture between the root and trunk of a tree should be planted at or evenly slightly above ground level.

Try not to disturb the roots when removing your olive tree from its container or burlap covering. Place the root ball in the prepared hole, and rotate as needed for an attractive appearance. Then backfill with either native soil or soil that has been only minimally changed, filling in the hole halfway. Press the soil down firmly and water thoroughly to settle the soil and eliminate air pockets. If the plant settles below the level of the surrounding soil, pump it up and down while the soil is saturated to raise the tree to the proper level. Finally, fill in the rest of the hole, tamp the earth down, and water thoroughly.

If you've purchased a bare-root olive tree, the planting technique will be somewhat different. After digging a hole just large enough to accommodate the roots, create a firm cone of soil at the bottom of the hole. Spread the roots of the tree over the cone, and hold the plant upright as you firm the soil around its roots. Backfill almost completely, with native soil or soil that's been only slightly changed, and water thoroughly to settle the soil around the roots and eliminate air pockets. If the plant settles below the level of the surrounding soil, pump it up and down while the soil is saturated to raise the tree to the proper level. Then finish filling the hole with soil, and water again.

Planting a Bare-Root
Olive Tree

Your olive tree will benefit from a protective layer of mulch placed around the tree to prevent the evaporation of water, to cool the soil, and to reduce the growth of weeds. Keep the mulch four to six inches away from the base of the tree to permit the tree to breathe. Over time, as the mulch decomposes, nutrients such as nitrogen will be transferred to the soil by earthworms, rain, and microorganisms. If you are planting in an area that has relatively long, cold, wet winters and short summers, mulch only lightly or not at all, as an excessive amount of mulch will conserve too much water.

Planting Your Tree in a Container

Olives grow exceptionally well in pots. Container-grown olive trees can develop into beautiful, robust plants, and can even bear fruit when their winter environment provides sufficiently chilly temperatures.

When selecting a container for your olive tree, choose a large planter, a half barrel, or another sizeable receptacle that has several drainage holes in the bottom. If necessary, drill additional holes using a hole saw drill attachment. Then, to further insure good drainage, cover the bottom of the container with several inches of gravel. Drainage can be improved even further with the use of a patio-and-tub potting mix.

Begin by partially filling the container with the potting mix. Place the olive tree inside the tub to get an idea of how it will look, and fill the pot with enough potting mix so that the juncture between the root and trunk of the tree will be planted at or slightly above soil level. When the tree is properly positioned, add more potting soil as needed until the tree is planted securely in the container.

Water the soil thoroughly to settle it around the roots and eliminate any air pockets. If the plant settles below the level of the surrounding soil,

If your area has frigid winter temperatures, you'll want to plant your olive tree in a pot. Fortunately, container-grown olive trees flourish, and can even provide a crop of olives as long as their winter environment is cool enough to set fruit.

Just like olive trees planted in your yard, container-grown trees require good drainage. For best results, drill additional holes, as necessary, in the bottom of the pot; add several inches of gravel; and use a patio-and-tub potting mixture.

pump it up and down while the soil is saturated to raise the tree to the proper level. Then finish filling the hole with the potting soil, and water again.

CARING FOR YOUR OLIVE TREE

In spite of the fact that olives flourish in the wild, they benefit from care and attention, including watering, fertilizing, pruning, and thinning.

As discussed earlier in the chapter, your olive tree can survive with very little water. If you're hoping for a crop of olives, though, regular watering will probably be necessary. There are many factors that can affect the water requirements of an olive tree, the foremost of which is annual rainfall. Soil type is another factor, with trees planted in sand requiring more frequent waterings than those growing in other types of soil. And local climate is yet another variable, as the more sun the tree is exposed to, the more water it will need.

In general, during the tree's first year, it should receive six to eight gallons of water per week. This amount will increase, however, as the tree grows. In hot climates, two to three waterings a week is necessary, especially if the soil is light and sandy. Just be sure that the soil is at least 75 percent dry before each watering, as olive trees are highly susceptible to crown rot. Insert your finger a couple of inches into the soil to determine if the earth is dry.

Fertilizers can greatly enhance an olive tree's health and productivity. Traditionally, fertilizing has always been accomplished with well-rotted manures. This insures that all nutrients are readily usable by the trees; reduces the possibility of over-fertilizing, which can harm the tree; and releases the nutrients slowly so that nutrient levels remain steady throughout the season. It is essential that these manures be rotted, as fresh manure

Olives at Monticello

Thomas Jefferson (1743–1826), the third President of the United States, was enamored of the olive, referring to it as "the richest gift of heaven, one of the most precious productions in nature," and "the most interesting plant in existence." For many years, Jefferson attempted to establish an olive grove at Monticello, the estate that Jefferson designed and built. In a 1778 entry in his Garden Book, Jefferson wrote about one of his many attempts to cultivate the tree:

Brought an olive tree from Colle [an Italian farmer-philosopher who owned an adjacent farm]. It is a shoot from an old root, being one of many brought from Italy in 1773. They stood the winter of that year and the remarkable frost of May 5, 1774, also the winters of 1774 & 1775, planted in the open field & without any cover. In Decemb. 1775 & Jan. 1776, there was a frost of four or five weeks duration, the earth being frozen like a rock the whole time. This killed all the olives; the others totally, this one alone sprung up from the old root. Its height now is 21¾. Took a cutting from it & planted it.

The harsh winters of Virginia proved too severe for Jefferson's olives. None of his trees lived long. But the story of Monticello's olives does not end with Jefferson's death. In 1993, Peter Hatch, the Director of Gardens and Grounds at Monticello, was given an olive tree to adorn Jefferson's home. Although at first the tree thrived, producing nearly twenty gallons of olives in one growing season, a harsh winter soon left the tree stone dead. Again, Monticello was bereft of olives.

Fortunately for Monticello's many visitors, the staff soon realized that olives can survive in Virginia—as long as they are grown in containers and brought inside each winter. Now, says Hatch, they have found that olives "make the handsomest of potted trees with their cooling silvery-white canopy, the compact leaves nodding in a summer breeze like silent chimes." And, after experiments that spanned more than two centuries, Monticello is graced with the beauty of the olive tree.

can actually burn the roots of the tree. Of course, chemical fertilizers can also be used to nourish your olive tree, and, in fact, are generally less expensive and easier to apply than manures. However, their use must be carefully monitored to avoid excessive applications. Your local nursery should be able to guide you in the selection and proper use of fertilizers for your tree. Many experts suggest Miracle Grow or an all-purpose 16-16-16 (Triple Sixteen) fertilizer to keep olive trees strong and productive from year to year.

Like watering and fertilizing, pruning is not needed if you merely want your olive tree to survive. If, however, you want a vigorous tree capable of bearing fruit, careful pruning is a must. Pruning insures that the tree will be easy to harvest, with the fruit distributed within reach over the outside shell of the entire tree. Judicious pruning also helps control the size and quality of the fruit, and guarantees a succession of crops.

Young trees should be pruned in the spring, with another pruning in mid-summer. The idea is to eliminate unwanted branches before they have a chance to develop fully. Prune to create a basic framework of three healthy "scaffold" branches, that will themselves branch out and bear fruit as the tree grows. The ideal shape of a bearing olive tree is rounded and low to the ground.

Fruit develops on shoots put forth the previous season, not on old wood. That means that the bearing area of *Olea europaea* is actually a shell of from two to three feet deep. Any fruit that does set in the interior of the tree is disappointing and not worth harvesting. Appropriate pruning insures a continuing supply of new fruiting wood. It also helps keep the bearing area of the tree in healthy condition.

Mature trees should also be pruned, not only for all the reasons given above, but also because cutting away extraneous branches stimulates the growth of new fruiting wood. Any dead or dying twigs in the productive shell should be removed. The hemispheric bearing shell of the tree also should be thinned to insure that the fruiting wood will get enough sun.

Your crop will be further improved if you thin the fruit as necessary. The ideal fruit set is about three to five olives for every foot of bearing twig. If you find yourself with an olive tree that is loaded with fruit, after your initial delight, you may face disappointment. First, the olives will be small, and, second, the tree may be so worn out that it will fail to bear the following year. For best growth and a good harvest, hand-thin your fruits in late spring to early summer, stripping off all but three to five olives for every foot of fruit set. Be ruthless. Unless you take off enough of the excess fruit, you won't benefit from thinning.

UNDERSTANDING THE HARVEST

Under ideal conditions and with tender loving care, an olive tree will start bearing fruit in its fourth or fifth year. Because a tree purchased from a nursery is generally between one and three years old when you plant it, it might not take as long as you think to reach maturity. Once your very own *Olea europaea* begins to bear, each year thereafter, it will set more olives than the year before. However, if you're looking for instant gratification, you won't get it from this ancient species. An olive tree won't be fully productive until it's twenty to thirty-five years old.

In southern California, where I live, the olive groves are usually in full bloom in the spring, from early May to the beginning of June. The first faint hint that an olive tree is preparing to bloom occurs when buds come forth, but it takes about eight weeks after that before the flowers appear. Flowering usually occurs on branches that were formed the previous season, but blossoms can actually appear from dormant buds that are a year or two old.

Be ruthless when thinning the fruit on your olive tree. If more than three to five olives are allowed to grow per foot, the olives will be disappointingly small, and the tree may be too exhausted to produce a crop the following year.

Although olive trees can start bearing fruit in their fourth or fifth year, surprisingly, they often don't reach full maturity and productivity until their thirty-fifth year. Once this stage is reached, though, productivity can remain strong for well over a century!

As explained in Chapter 2, the olive tree has two kinds of flowers. The perfect flower has both male and female parts—the stamen and the pistil—while the staminate flower has only the stamen, and lacks the part necessary for fruiting. Only perfect flowers will set fruit, with each flower developing into one olive. A tree that bears poorly may be burdened with an excess of staminate flowers and have few perfect flowers.

Some olive trees bear fruit only every other year. A non-bearing year usually occurs after a year of exceptionally heavy fruiting. In such instances, the stalwart tree has most likely exhausted its nutrient reserves during the bearing season and can't quite recoup by the next. Regular watering and fertilization helps to promote more consistent annual yields.

Once olives appear on your tree during the late spring, you will be encouraged by the rapid growth seen throughout their first stage of development. The second stage, which comes in late summer and early fall, brings slower growth; while the third stage, which arrives in mid-fall, is another period of rapid growth. By now, the olives are looking fat and happy. If not harvested during this time, expect another period of slow growth with the fruit increasing in size, probably due to an extra accumulation of the golden oil. Keep in mind that healthy fruit is dependent on an adequate supply of water. When there's not enough moisture in the soil, the leaves will steal water from the fruit and you'll end up with very unattractive shriveled olives.

Fruit destined to be cured for table olives is ready for the harvest anywhere from mid-September to early November. Use the squeeze test. A mature, ready-to-pick olive will release a white juice when pressed between the thumb and finger. You'll also know that your olives are fully ripe when a few naturally fall from the tree. When you're ready to harvest, strip the mature olives from the tree by hand. Be gentle, lest your precious fruit be bruised.

If you judge that your olives are too small for canning, consider having them pressed for their delicious oil. (The Olive Oil Source, included in the Resource List on page 186, can help you track down companies that will press your crop into oil, as well as companies that sell olive presses suitable for home use.) Olives that are meant to be extracted should remain on the tree until they become completely black. The longer they remain on the tree, the more oil they will contain. If frost is not a factor, olives can stay on the tree until as late as mid-February.

Hopefully, you now are the proud owner of a beautiful, healthy olive tree. Perhaps you're even revelling in a crop of plump olives. If so, you may want to turn to Chapter 6, where you'll learn how to turn your home-grown fruit into succulent tidbits, delicious enough to rival the olives in any specialty store. Or, if you prefer, turn to Chapter 7, where you'll find a wealth of olive recipes, from the classic martini to Easy Olive Tapenade. Either way, you're sure to learn new ways of enjoying the sophisticated olive.

When should your olives be harvested? Fruit destined for curing should be picked anywhere from mid-September to early November. If you intend to press your olives for oil, though, wait until the fruit turns black—even as late as mid-February.

PART TWO

The **Tastes** &**Pleasures** of the **Olive**

CHAPTER 6

The **Art** of **Olive** Making

The whole Mediterranean . . . seems to rise in the sour, pungent smell of these black olives between the teeth. A taste older than meat, older than wine. A taste as old as cold water.

—LAWRENCE DURRELL (1912–1990)

As you have already learned, olives are hard and bitter fresh off the tree. During the curing process, though, the fruit magically develops a mellow richness, with a distinctive flavor and a tender flesh. You may very well prefer to buy your olives ready-made. But if your olive tree has provided you with a bumper crop of plump fruit—or if you'd simply like to try your hand at an age-old process—this chapter provides all the information you need to produce jars of delicious home-cured olives.

Of course, while the olive variety you choose will help determine the character of the finished product, your method of home-curing will have

Working With Lye

Several of the recipes in this chapter—Green Olives, Spanish-Style Green Olives, and Black Olives—use lye in the curing process. Why? Lye leaches out the bitter compound found in olives, leaving them rich and delicious.

If you have never worked with lye before, you may find the idea a little frightening. The fact is that lye has been used for hundreds of years, not only to cure olives but also in the soap-making process. Flake lye is, in fact, readily available in cans in most supermarkets. Nevertheless, if you think that lye is potentially dangerous, you're right. Lye is a caustic substance that can cause nasty burns if splashed on the skin, and can result in serious injury or death if swallowed. However, by following the precautions listed below, you'll be able to use lye without mishap and fully enjoy the olive-making process.

❏ When working with lye, always wear protective clothing, including forearm-length rubber gloves, safety goggles, long sleeves, closed shoes, and socks.

❏ Always slowly add lye to the water with which it's being mixed. Never pour water or any other substance onto lye, as it can cause a violent reaction.

❏ Use only cold water when preparing your lye solution. Be aware that when mixed with water, lye causes a chemical reaction that results in heat. Make sure to cool the solution to 65°F to 70°F before adding the olives. Olives immersed in a hot bath will become unpleasantly mushy as they cure.

❏ Make sure that the room in which you're working is well ventilated. Open the window and turn on the fan if you have one. Be aware that lye fumes can damage your lungs. The best way to avoid this is to keep the air moving!

❏ When mixing any lye solution, use only stainless steel or ceramic containers. Never use glass or aluminum, as glass can explode and aluminum can cause a chemical reaction. Plastic, also, is not recommended. If you're lucky enough to have a heavy stoneware crock on hand, by all means use it. That is what housewives used centuries ago.

❏ Use long-handled wooden spoons to stir your lye solution, and wash them thoroughly with hot soapy water after each use. Don't use these utensils for anything other than working with lye.

❏ Keep children and animals away from lye, locking them out of the room if you have to.

❏ Always keep a bottle of vinegar handy, and if any lye falls on your skin, quickly rinse the area with vinegar, which will neutralize the lye. If any lye gets in your eye, immediately pour large amounts of cool water into your eye for ten minutes or longer. Then seek medical care. If lye is accidentally swallowed, do not induce vomiting. Instead, call a poison control center or 911 for further instructions.

❏ Store your lye in an airtight, clearly labelled container, well out of the reach of children and curious pets. Store it only in its dry form. Never store lye in solution.

❏ To safely dispose of a lye solution, carefully pour it into the toilet and flush twice to clear the pipes and prevent any possible backsplash. Keep in mind that the solution poses no danger to your pipes. In fact, lye is used in quite a number of commercial drain cleaners.

an effect as well. You can produce rich and mellow black olives, tangy green olives, salty olives, or even hot and spicy olives. Each recipe in this chapter begins with a description of the finished product, making it easy to pick the technique that will best suit your tastes.

Although olive lovers have home-cured the fruit of the olive tree for thousands of years, keep in mind that care should be taken when preparing and storing your olives. If your chosen method of curing includes lye, be sure to take the proper precautions when handling this substance. (For details, see the inset on page 96.) Also be aware that the olive recipes in this chapter do not include chemical preservatives or heat processing. Thus, your homemade olives should be eaten within the time period stated in the recipe, and should be promptly discarded if they show any signs of spoilage. (See the inset on page 109.)

Home-curing takes time and patience, but the results are well worth the effort. Whether you're using fruit from your own trees or you're working with store-bought produce, the final luscious treats are sure to give you a greater appreciation of the sophisticated olive.

GREEN OLIVES

For this recipe, choose olives that are green, straw-colored, or red. Don't use tree-ripened black olives, because they will be soft and mushy when cured. Expect your cured olives to be similar to green supermarket olives—firm-fleshed with a mildly tangy taste. It's best to start curing these olives early in the morning. Ideally, it takes ten to twelve hours for the lye solution to fully penetrate the olive flesh, so if you start early in the day, there's an excellent chance the curing will be complete by bedtime. However, if the olives are very green, curing may take as long as thirty hours.

1. Wearing rubber gloves, make Lye Solution #1 by placing the cold water in a large stainless steel or ceramic container. (Do not use glass, aluminum, or plastic.) Slowly add the lye to the water, and stir with a large wooden spoon until dissolved. Remember that the lye will generate heat, and set the solution aside to cool to 65°F to 70°F.

2. With gloves on, carefully slide the olives into the solution, making sure that they are completely covered. Half fill a heavy-duty plastic kitchen trash bag with water, and secure with a twist tie. Then place the water-filled bag on top of the olives to make sure that they remain completely immersed in the lye solution. If necessary, place a plate on top of the water-filled bag to weigh it down.

3. With gloves on, stir the olives every 2 or 3 hours. For the curing to be successful, the lye solution must reach the pits. To test the amount of penetration, carefully take out one of the largest olives and cut it down to the pit. The lye solution causes the flesh of the olive to take on a yellow-green color. If the color isn't even, the olives are not ready.

YIELD: 2 POUNDS CURED GREEN OLIVES

2 pounds fresh green, straw-colored, or red olives, unpitted

LYE SOLUTION #1

2 quarts cold water

2 tablespoons household lye

LYE SOLUTION #2

1 gallon cold water

2 tablespoons household lye

BRINE

3 tablespoons salt

2 quarts water

4. If the olives aren't cured by bedtime, carefully discard the lye solution by flushing it down the toilet, and cover the olives with cold water. In the morning, prepare Lye Solution #2 as directed in Step 1. Discard the water the olives were soaking in overnight, and cover them with the lye solution, as directed in Step 2.

5. Follow Step 3, stirring every 2 or 3 hours. Test the amount of penetration by cutting open an olive, as directed earlier.

6. When it's apparent that the lye has fully penetrated the flesh of the olive, carefully discard the lye solution. Rinse the olives twice in cold water; then cover them with fresh cold water, being careful to avoid exposing the olives to the air any longer than you must while changing the water. (Air will cause the fruit to darken.) Submerge the olives fully in the water to exclude all air, following the procedure described in Step 2.

7. To leach the lye solution out of the olives, change the water 4 times each day. This part of the curing process is complete when you can no longer detect a hint of bitterness when the olives are tasted. It may take as long as 7 or 8 days to completely remove all the lye.

8. Before discarding the last rinse water, prepare the brine by dissolving the salt in the water. Cover the olives with the solution by using the procedure described in Step 2, and let the olives rest in the brine for 2 days.

9. After their salt-soak, the olives are ready to eat. Store them in the refrigerator completely submerged in the brine, and gobble them up within 2 weeks. If you wish, you may store the olives in glass jars.

SPANISH-STYLE GREEN OLIVES

These luscious olives have green skin and a tender light green flesh. The distinctive flavor and aroma come from lactic-acid fermentation, which is what makes them so appealing. Any variety of olive is suitable, but the best are Sevillano and Manzanilla. (See Chapter 3.) Select unblemished olives that are green to yellow in color, and try to keep them uniform in size.

1. Wearing rubber gloves, make the lye solution by placing the cold water in a large stainless steel or ceramic container. (Do not use glass, aluminum, or plastic.) Slowly add the lye to the water, and stir with a large wooden spoon until dissolved. Remember that the lye will generate heat, and set the solution aside to cool to 65°F to 70°F.

2. With gloves on, carefully slide the olives into the solution, making sure that they are completely covered. Half fill a heavy-duty plastic kitchen trash bag with water, and secure with a twist tie. Then place the water-filled bag on top of the olives to make sure that they remain completely immersed in the lye solution. If necessary, place a plate on top of the water-filled bag to weigh it down.

3. Allow the lye to penetrate the flesh of the olives about three-fourths of the way to the pit. To test the amount of penetration, carefully take out one of the largest olives and cut it down to the pit. The lye solution causes the flesh of the olive to take on a yellow-green color. If the color hasn't penetrated far enough, the olives are not ready. This soaking may take from 4 to 6 days.

4. When it's apparent that the lye has adequately penetrated the flesh of the olives, carefully discard the lye solution by flushing it down the toilet. Rinse the olives twice in cold water; then cover them with fresh

---

YIELD: 2 POUNDS CURED GREEN OLIVES

2 pounds fresh green or yellow olives, unpitted

LYE SOLUTION

2 quarts cold water

2 tablespoons household lye

BRINE

8 ounces salt

2 quarts water

LACTIC-ACID BOOSTER

3 ounces dill pickle or sauerkraut juice

3/4 teaspoon sugar, or 1 teaspoon corn syrup

STORAGE CONTAINERS

Two 1-quart glass jars with lids

cold water, being careful to avoid exposing the olives to the air any longer than you must while changing the water. (Air will cause the fruit to darken.) Submerge the olives fully in the water to exclude all air, following the procedure described in Step 2.

5. To leach the lye solution out of the olives, change the water every 4 hours. This part of the curing process is complete when you can no longer detect a hint of bitterness when the olives are tasted. It will take from 1 to 2 days to completely remove all the lye.

6. Before discarding the last rinse water, prepare the brine by dissolving the salt in the water. Pack the washed and drained olives into the jars and cover with the brine. Put the lids on loosely. To hasten fermentation, store the olives in a place where the temperature is between 70°F and 90°F, but not over 100°F. Expect some frothing and foaming during this period of active fermentation, which will last from 4 to 5 days. The olives must stay submerged in the brine. If brine overflows, replace it with fresh brine.

7. When the brine has stopped foaming, prepare the lactic-acid booster by mixing the pickle or sauerkraut juice with the sugar or corn syrup. (The sugar or corn syrup is added to feed the bacteria.) Divide the booster equally between the jars and stir into the brine, being careful not to bruise the olives in the process. Cap loosely and let rest for about a week.

8. By the sixth or seventh day, gas production will be slower, although fermentation will continue. Be sure the jars are topped off with brine. Firmly tighten the lids to exclude air, and let the olives rest in a cool place until ready to serve, at least another 3 days. Use the olives within 2 weeks.

BLACK OLIVES

Like the black olives produced in California, these morsels start life as unripe fruit. Choose olives that are green, straw-colored, or cherry red, and are of the same color and the same approximate size. This procedure is more complex and time-consuming than that used to make green olives, but the rich and mellow treats it yields have incomparable flavor and texture.

1. On the first day, wearing rubber gloves, make Lye Solution #1 by placing the cold water in a large stainless steel or ceramic container. (Do not use glass, aluminum, or plastic.) Slowly add the lye to the water, and stir with a large wooden spoon until dissolved. Remember that the lye will generate heat, and set the solution aside to cool to 65°F to 70°F.

2. With gloves on, carefully slide the olives into the solution, making sure that they are completely covered. They need not be weighed down.

3. Allow the lye to penetrate only the skin of the olives. Check after 3 hours, and then every 30 minutes, by cutting open an olive and examining the color. The lye solution causes the olive to take on a yellow-green color.

4. When sufficient penetration has been achieved, carefully discard the lye solution by flushing it down the toilet. Allow the olives to remain in the soaking container, exposed to the air. This helps give the olives their dark color. Stir 3 times during the day.

5. On the second day, prepare another batch of Lye Solution #1, following the directions in Step 1.

YIELD: **2 POUNDS** CURED BLACK OLIVES

2 pounds fresh green, straw-colored, or red olives, unpitted

LYE SOLUTION #1*

2 quarts cold water

1 1/2 tablespoons household lye

LYE SOLUTION #2

2 quarts cold water

2 tablespoons household lye

BRINE

3 tablespoons salt

2 quarts water

* Note that you will have to mix a new batch of Lye Solution #1 for each of the first four days.

6. Slide the olives into the solution as directed in Step 2, and allow to soak until the solution has penetrated $1/32$ to $1/16$ of the way into the flesh. Check after 3 hours, and then every 30 minutes, by cutting open an olive and examining the color.

7. When sufficient penetration has been achieved, discard the lye solution, following the instructions in Step 4.

8. On the third day, prepare another batch of Lye Solution #1, following the directions in Step 1.

9. Slide the olives into the solution as directed in Step 2, and allow to soak until the solution has penetrated $1/8$ to $3/16$ of the way into the flesh. Check after 3 hours, and then every 30 minutes, by cutting open an olive and examining the color.

10. When sufficient penetration has been achieved, carefully discard the lye solution, following the instructions in Step 4.

11. On the fourth day, prepare another batch of Lye Solution #1, following the directions in Step 1.

12. Slide the olives into the solution as directed in Step 2, and allow to soak until the solution has penetrated $5/16$ of the way into the flesh. Check after 3 hours, and then every 30 minutes, by cutting open an olive and examining the color.

13. When sufficient penetration has been achieved, discard the lye solution, following the instructions in Step 4.

14. On the fifth day, prepare Lye Solution #2, following the directions in Step 1.

15. Slide the olives into the solution as directed in Step 2, and allow to soak until the solution has penetrated the flesh completely and reached the pit. Check after 3 hours, and then every 30 minutes, by cutting open an olive and examining the color.

16. When sufficient penetration has been achieved, carefully discard the lye solution, following the instructions in Step 4.

17. To leach the lye solution out of the olives, change the water 4 times each day. This part of the curing process is complete when you can no longer detect a hint of bitterness when the olives are tasted. It may take as long as 7 or 8 days to completely remove all the lye.

18. When the olives are cleansed of lye, prepare the brine by dissolving the salt in the water. Cover the olives with the brine, and let the olives rest in the brine for 2 days.

19. After their salt-soak, the olives are ready to eat. Store them in the refrigerator completely submerged in the brine, and gobble them up within 2 weeks. If you wish, you may store the olives in glass jars.

DRY SALT-CURED OLIVES

YIELD: 2 POUNDS
CURED BLACK OLIVES

2 pounds small fresh dark red or nearly black olives, unpitted

CURING SALT

1 pound salt

2 additional pounds salt for top layer

STORING SALT

2 ounces salt
($1/4$ cup)

CURING CONTAINER

18-x-18-inch clean wooden box

2–4 yards clean burlap

Olives cured by the dry salt method are very salty and somewhat bitter. Because the salt draws out moisture, these olives have a wrinkled appearance. I find them delicious, but if you've never had olives cured in salt, you may find them a bit too salty for your taste. Select mature olives that are dark red or almost black. Mission olives are the variety of choice, but all olives work well. Use small-sized olives when curing with salt, as large olives get too soft.

1. To make the curing container, line the wooden box with the burlap.

2. Place the 1 pound of curing salt and the 2 pounds of olives in the box, and toss to mix. To keep mold from forming, move the olives around to be sure they are well coated with the salt. Pour the additional 2 pounds of salt evenly over the olives. The top layer of salt should reach a depth of 1 inch. The salt will combine with the moisture from the olives to produce a brine, so keep the box outside in a protected place, as it may leak.

3. After 1 week, the olives must be rearranged. Pour the olives and salt into another container, and then back into the prepared box. Let them rest for 3 days and then mix again.

4. Every 3 days thereafter, repeat the mixing process by turning the olives and salt into another container, and then putting all back in the original box. Follow this step until the olives are shriveled and well-cured. This part of the process will take from 30 to 36 days. A taste test will tell you when the olives are ready.

5. Discard the excess salt by gently shaking the olives in a colander. Because all of the olives probably won't fit in the colander, do this step in stages.

6. Fill a large pot with water, and bring to a boil. Quickly dip the olives in the boiling water. To make this easy, use a pot large enough to accommodate the colander, and dip the olive-filled colander in and out of the water.

7. Drain the olives on a large towel or on several layers of paper towels. Allow to air dry overnight.

8. Mix the dried olives with the 2 ounces of storing salt, and place in an airtight container. Store in the refrigerator, and use within a month. These olives may be used as is in cooking. If you want to munch on them, spray them with olive oil and roll them around to give them an appetizing shine and extra flavor.

YIELD: 2 POUNDS
CURED BLACK OLIVES

2 pounds fresh dark
red or black olives,
unpitted

BRINE SOLUTION #I

4 ounces salt
(¹/₂ cup)

2 quarts water

BRINE SOLUTION #2*

8 ounces salt
(I cup)

2 quarts water

STORAGE
CONTAINERS

Two I-quart glass
jars with lids

*Note that you will have to
mix a new batch of Brine
Solution #2 for the second
and third stages of the
curing process.

BRINE-CURED OLIVES

*To make these salty, tangy olives, select mature fruit that is
dark red to purple or even black in color, and firm in texture. Manzanilla
and Mission olives are your best bets.
Because of the salty brine, these olives may be shriveled.
Be aware that some may fade in color during curing,
but will probably darken again when exposed to air.*

1. Prepare Brine Solution #1 by completely dissolving the salt in the water.

2. Divide the olives evenly between the 2 jars, and cover completely with the brine. Fasten the lids loosely, and store the jars in a cool place (between 60°F and 70°F) for 1 week.

3. After 1 week, prepare Brine Solution #2 by completely dissolving the salt in the water. Discard the old brine and fill the jars with the new brine. Again, store in a cool place, this time for 2 weeks.

4. After 2 weeks, prepare another batch of Brine Solution #2. Discard the old brine and again fill the jars with the new brine. This time, fasten the lids securely. Store in a cool place for 2 months, keeping close watch. If pressure forms, loosen the lids to release the gas, and then close the jars firmly again. If the brine spews out at any time, open the lids carefully, discard the brine, and replace it with a new batch of Brine Solution #2.

5. The salty brine will preserve the olives for about a year, as long as the container is airtight and the olives are immersed in the brine. These

olives may be used as is in cooking. If you want to munch on them, soak them overnight in cool water to eliminate excess salt. Any soaked olives that are not immediately eaten can be stored in a solution of one part red wine and one part red wine vinegar. Float a layer of olive oil on the surface and refrigerate. Bring to room temperature before serving.

When Good Olives Turn Bad

Once cured, your homemade olives will stay fresh for two weeks to a year, depending on the curing process used. Be aware, though, that all home-preserved foodstuffs pose the potential threat of botulism, and that low-acid foods such as olives are particularly at risk. That's the bad news. The good news is that botulism—a form of food poisoning caused by the bacteria Clostridium botulinum—is relatively rare, and that harmful olives are easy to detect. To avoid problems in both homemade and commercial olives, be sure to follow these simple guidelines:

❏ If your olives are stored in brine, make sure that they are completely submerged in the liquid. The salt in the brine will help prevent spoilage. Then keep the container in a cool place—preferably, in the refrigerator.

❏ Discard any olives that develop a rancid or foul odor, show signs of mold, or are discolored.

❏ Discard any olives whose jars have bulging, rusted, or corroded lids.

❏ Once the fermentation process is complete, discard any olives whose jars have liquid oozing from under the lid or that spurt liquid or foam when the container is opened.

❏ If you or anyone else shows signs of botulism—including blurred or double vision, general weakness, poor reflexes, or difficulty swallowing or breathing—promptly seek medical attention. Botulism requires professional care.

YIELD: 2 POUNDS
CURED GREEN OLIVES

2 pounds fresh
green olives,
unpitted

BRINE

4 ounces salt
(½ cup)

2 quarts water

4 pints white vinegar

SEASONINGS

2 tablespoons
pickling spice

1 tablespoon fennel
seed

2 cloves garlic

2 small hot red
peppers

2 sprigs fresh dill

10 peppercorns

**STORAGE
CONTAINERS**

Two 1-quart glass
jars with rubber
seals and lids

HOT AND SPICY SICILIAN-STYLE OLIVES

*Cured in a spicy brine, these olives are a bit bitter,
but undeniably delicious. Any variety of unblemished fresh
green olives can be used to make these Sicilian-style treats,
but Sevillano are the traditional choice.*

1. To prepare the brine, completely dissolve the salt in the water. Then stir in the vinegar, blending thoroughly.

2. Divide the olives evenly between the 2 jars. Add half of each of the seasonings to each jar, and follow with half of the brine. Fasten the lids loosely, and store the jars in a cool place (between 60°F and 70°F) for 2 months. If the brine spews out at any time, open the lid carefully and replace it with enough of the salt-and-vinegar brine to cover the olives.

3. After about 2 months, gas production and fermentation will stop. Seal the jars tightly and store in a cool place until the olives are mellow and have the desired flavor. The entire curing process will take from 4 to 6 months. The brine will preserve the olives for about a year, as long as the container is airtight and the olives are immersed in the brine.

CHAPTER 7

CookingWith Olives&OliveOil

*Her acidic bons mots were the olives
of the martini age.*

—*VANITY FAIR* on Dorothy Parker, June 1986

Perhaps, following the directions in Chapter 6, you've just cured your own delicious olives. Or maybe you've simply stocked your pantry with some wonderful jars of store-bought olives. It goes without saying that these luscious globes are a treat in and of themselves. But if you're a true olive lover, you won't want to stop there, because there are so many truly scrumptious dishes that can be made not only with the olive, but also with its golden oil. This chapter explores the wide variety of dishes that you can create—for yourself, for your family, or for your admiring guests.

In honor of the wondrous fruit to which this book is dedicated, this chapter includes everything "olive." In the following pages, you'll find recipes for classic drinks such as The Perfect Dry Martini; enticing appetizers such as Easy Olive Tapenade; savory sauces such as piquant Rémoulade; satisfying entrées such as Mediterranean Vegetable Bake; and hearty breads such as Old-Fashioned Olive Bread. You'll even find tempting baked sweets made with olive oil. Baking with olive oil may seem a bit unusual, but I promise you'll love everything you make. Not only are baked goods healthier when prepared with olive oil, but they stay moist and delicious for a very long time.

Almost any olive will enhance any dish, so for the most part, I haven't specified a particular variety in the recipes that follow, although I have usually specified whether the olives should be black or green. Similarly, in most cases, I haven't specified a particular olive oil. If you're planning on making some infused olive oils (see page 130), you may want to use one of your own creations. If you have no flavored oils on hand, though, just choose the best quality olive oil you have in your pantry. (For more information on this, see the inset on page 126.)

One final note is in order. Olives should be pitted when they're used in a recipe. There's nothing worse than crunching down on an unexpected pit! To easily pit an olive, turn it on its side on a cutting board and smash it lightly with the side of a chef's knife. Then squeeze, and the pit will pop out.

So the next time you yearn for a delectable snack or a truly memorable main course, just flip through these pages, and delight in the sophisticated olive.

COCKTAILS AND PARTY FARE

THE PERFECT DRY MARTINI

Although martinis are often served "on the rocks," the traditional martini is "shaken, not stirred," in the words of James Bond. The Perfect Dry Martini would definitely please Mr. Bond.

1. Place $1/2$ to 1 cup of cracked ice in a shaker. Add the gin or vodka and the vermouth, and shake well. Strain into martini glasses, adding a dash of orange bitters to each glass, if desired.

2. Spear each olive with a toothpick. Drop one perfect olive into the bottom of each glass, and serve with pride.

YIELD: **4** MARTINIS

7 jiggers gin or vodka ($10^{1}/_2$ ounces)

2 jiggers vermouth (3 ounces)

Dash orange bitters (optional)

4 large green pimento-stuffed olives

THE DIRTY MARTINI

Dirty martinis are exceedingly popular among olive aficionados. That's because the extra soupçon of olive brine adds immensely to the flavor. You may use the "juice" from a bottle of olives, or opt for a special dirty martini mix. (If the mix isn't available in your market, check out the Resource List on page 185.)

1. Place $1/2$ to 1 cup of cracked ice in a shaker. Add the gin or vodka and the vermouth, plus the brine or dirty martini mix. Shake well and strain into martini glasses.

2. Spear each olive with a toothpick. Drop one perfect olive into the bottom of each glass, and serve with pride.

YIELD: **4** MARTINIS

7 jiggers gin or vodka ($10^{1}/_2$ ounces)

2 jiggers vermouth (3 ounces)

1 jigger olive brine or dirty martini mix ($1^{1}/_2$ ounces)

4 large olives of your choice

The Martini's Finishing Touch

No book about olives would be complete without a mention of the martini. Who can imagine a martini without an olive? Yes, I know that there are those who take their martini with a twist of lemon, but we won't speak of that sacrilege here.

There are several accounts of how the legendary martini got its name. Some say it happened during the California Gold Rush in the late 1870s. It seems that a tipsy miner who had stumbled on a rich strike wanted to celebrate with a drink that no one had ever enjoyed before. The miner offered an extraordinarily large gold nugget to any bartender in the saloon who could come up with something special. The challenge was met by Julio Richelieu, who poured a healthy slug of gin, swirled in some vermouth, added an olive, and ceremoniously offered it to the miner. When the drink was greeted with a smack of approval, he was awarded the gold nugget. Julio christened the cocktail the martinez, after the California city in which it was first served. Over time, the name became slurred often enough by those who over-imbibed that it turned into the martini.

Others say that John D. Rockefeller was the first to taste this now-familiar combination of gin and vermouth. According to the story, it was Martini di Arona di Taggia, tending bar with a Latin flourish, who devised the drink and served it to Rockefeller in 1910 at New York's Knickerbocker Hotel. It's been reported that John D. himself named this cocktail after his favorite bartender.

No matter who came up with the inspired combination of alcohol and olive, it's a fact that the martini first made its rounds in the Roaring Twenties. Flappers with marcelled hair danced the night away with their dapper beaus, sometimes with a martini in hand. It's no wonder those times were called "roaring." The martini is a potent potion.

Prohibition against alcohol became law after World War I, when the Eighteenth Amendment passed, but it hardly slowed things down. Martinis remained popular, olives were easy to come by, and bathtub gin was in. When Prohibition was repealed in 1933, sophisticates openly celebrated, glass in hand. The glass, more often than not, was decorated with an olive on a toothpick.

At the Teheran Conference in late November of 1943, a debonair Franklin Delano Roosevelt served dirty martinis to his fellow conferees, Winston Churchill and Joseph Stalin. In case you don't know, a dirty martini is composed of gin or vodka, plus a splash of brine from a jar of olives. Instead of crystal clear, the drink turns cloudy. An olive is dropped in, of course. With that double dose of olive flavor, the dirty martini is doubly delicious. (Page 113 provides recipes for both a classic martini and a dirty martini.)

While the twenties introduced the martini, it was not until the fifties that the martini became the staple of the "cocktail hour." Sophisticated folks purchased cocktail shakers and distinctive Y-shaped martini glasses, and served ice-cold martinis to their stylish friends. Although the two-martini lunch was legendary in the sixties and seventies, the martini then briefly fell out of fashion—until the 1990s, when it came back with a roar. Now, you can find martinis not only in restaurants but also in bars devoted to the drink. And although some versions of the cocktail are trendy fruit-flavored concoctions, others are the classic gin-and-vermouth combination—adorned, of course, with the sophisticated olive.

JESSICA'S SPECIAL STUFFED OLIVES

My eleven-year-old grand-niece, Kalah, has a friend named Jessica who loves olives as much as I do. This is Jessica's recipe, reprinted here with her permission. These stuffed olives are easy to put together and truly scrumptious!

YIELD: 24 APPETIZERS

¼ cup grated Cheddar cheese

2 tablespoons grated white onion

24 pitted black olives

1. Place the grated cheese in a small bowl, and sprinkle with the grated onion. Toss with a fork to combine.

2. Tuck a pinch of the cheese mixture into the hollow of each olive, poking it in with your fingers.

3. Pile the stuffed olives in a pretty bowl, and serve immediately.

YIELD: 1 POUND
SPICY OLIVES

1 pound olives of
your choice

MARINADE

1 1/2 cups olive oil

1/4 cup white wine

1/4 cup water

2 cloves garlic,
minced

SEASONINGS

2 hot peppers

2 bay leaves

1 small bunch fresh
thyme

1 tablespoon minced
fresh rosemary

SPICY MARINATED OLIVES

For a real kick, add some of these hot and spicy olives to your party tray.
Easy to prepare, these treats are always a favorite with guests.

1. Place all of the marinade ingredients in a small saucepan, and heat just to the boiling point. Remove from the heat, cover, and set aside for 30 minutes.

2. Place the olives in a colander and rinse well. Pat the olives dry and set aside.

3. Pour the warm marinade into a clean 1 1/2-quart glass jar. Add the seasonings, cover, and shake well. Add the olives, and shake again.

4. Allow the olives to marinate at room temperature for 5 hours. Refrigerate if not serving immediately. If kept refrigerated, marinated olives will keep for about a month. Bring to room temperature and drain off the marinade before serving.

CHEESE BITE SURPRISE

YIELD: 24 APPETIZERS

Everyone loves puffy cheese bites, but I guarantee that everyone will like these even more. A wonderful cheese dough surrounds your favorite olives. If you want to make these savory treats a few days before the party, just freeze them and pop them into the oven 20 minutes before serving.

1 cup shredded Cheddar cheese

2 tablespoons olive oil

1/2 cup all-purpose flour

1/8–1/4 teaspoon cayenne pepper

24 olives of your choice (pimento-stuffed green olives are especially good)

1. Place the shredded cheese in a medium-sized bowl, and drizzle with the olive oil. Toss to combine.

2. Sift the flour and cayenne pepper directly onto the cheese mixture. Use the back of a fork to blend well.

3. Dry the olives slightly by rolling them around on a paper towel. This will help the dough adhere better. Mold a scant tablespoon of dough around each olive, pressing together well.

4. Lightly coat a cookie sheet with olive oil cooking spray. Arrange the wrapped olives on the sheet, spacing them about 2 inches apart.

5. Bake in a preheated 400°F oven for 15 minutes, or until lightly browned. Serve immediately. If you prefer, freeze the unbaked bites in a single layer and, when solidly frozen, transfer to a zip-lock plastic bag. Bake the frozen bites in a preheated 400°F oven for about 20 minutes, or until lightly browned. Serve immediately.

BASIC BRUSCHETTA

YIELD: ABOUT 24 APPETIZERS

1 loaf French bread

2 cloves garlic, peeled

$\frac{1}{2}$ cup olive oil

6 firm ripe tomatoes, such as Roma or plum, thinly sliced

6 slices mozzarella cheese, cut into quarters

Salt and cracked pepper to taste

6 leaves fresh basil, shredded

Bruschetta has become wildly popular in recent years. If you haven't yet made these crunchy, flavorful delights, you're in for a treat. Bruschetta is a favorite with every member of my family. Serve it at your next party or, better yet, prepare it any time you're in the mood for a delicious (but healthy) indulgence.

1. Cut the bread into $\frac{3}{4}$-inch to 1-inch slices, and arrange in a single layer on a baking sheet. Toast under a preheated broiler until light golden brown. Then turn the slices over and lightly toast the other side. Rub one side liberally with the garlic, and brush with the olive oil.

2. Top each of the prepared slices of toast with tomato slices, overlapping as needed to fit. Top with a square of cheese, folding to fit if necessary. Sprinkle lightly with salt and pepper to taste.

3. Briefly place the bruschetta under the broiler to melt the cheese, warm the tomato, and recrisp the toast. Sprinkle with the basil and serve immediately.

SPINACH BRUSCHETTA WITH FETA CHEESE

This is a delicious and healthy variation on Basic Bruschetta—
another winner that both your guests and your family are sure to cheer.

1. Cut the bread into ¾-inch to 1-inch slices, and arrange in a single layer on a baking sheet. Toast under a preheated broiler until light golden brown. Then turn the slices over and lightly toast the other side. Rub one side liberally with the garlic, and brush with ½ cup of the olive oil.

2. Place 2 tablespoons of the remaining olive oil in a large skillet over medium-high heat. When the oil is hot, add the spinach and stir to coat. Cook, stirring constantly, for about 2 minutes, or until the spinach is wilted.

3. Combine the remaining 1 tablespoon of olive oil with the balsamic vinegar and drizzle over the cooked spinach, tossing to mix. Sprinkle the mixture with salt and cracked pepper to taste.

4. Divide the dressed spinach among the prepared slices of toast. Sprinkle evenly with the feta cheese and serve immediately, preferably while the spinach is still warm.

YIELD: ABOUT 24
APPETIZERS

I loaf French bread

2 cloves garlic, peeled

½ cup plus 3 tablespoons olive oil, divided

I pound fresh spinach, torn or coarsely chopped

I tablespoon balsamic vinegar

Salt and cracked pepper to taste

2 ounces feta cheese, crumbled (about ¾ cup)

YIELD: ABOUT
24 APPETIZERS

½ cup olive oil

2 cloves garlic, crushed

6 firm ripe tomatoes, such as Roma or plum, cut into small dice

½ teaspoon salt

6 leaves fresh basil, shredded

I package (10 ounces) melba toast, or 24 slices French bread, toasted

EASY BRUSCHETTA

*If you love bruschetta, but Basic Bruschetta (page 118) and
Spinach Bruschetta With Feta Cheese (page 119) seem too time-consuming
to prepare, this easy-to-make hors d'oeuvre is the answer.
Simply place a bowl of this savory mixture in the center of a platter,
surround the bowl with melba toast or crisped French bread slices,
and allow guests to make their own luscious appetizers.*

1. Place the olive oil and garlic in a large bowl, and stir to combine. Add the diced tomatoes and salt, and stir lightly. Cover and let stand at room temperature for 2 hours to allow the flavors to meld.

2. Stir in the basil and serve immediately, surrounding the bowl with the melba toast or French bread slices.

YIELD: ABOUT 1 CUP

½ cup pitted green olives

½ cup pitted black olives

2 cloves roasted garlic (see page 162)

2 teaspoons olive oil

EASY OLIVE TAPENADE

*Tapenade, a chunky spread, is one of my favorite party starters. A tapenade
is easy to make ahead and easy to serve—just surround it with crackers and
let your guests help themselves. For full flavor, serve at room temperature.*

1. Place all of the ingredients in a food processor, and pulse until well combined. The olives should be finely minced, but should not be as smooth as a purée. If you don't have a food processor, mince the olives by hand and combine with the remaining ingredients.

2. Serve at room temperature with crusty bread or any bland crunchy crackers. The tapenade itself is richly flavorful and should be the star of the show.

OLIVE OIL REFRIGERATOR PICKLES

YIELD: 2 QUARTS

There are many ways of making pickles.
This is an especially delicious variation.
To impress guests, include these savory treats
on your next antipasto platter.

24 small cucumbers, each 3 to 4 inches long

½ cup coarse salt

2 small onions, thinly sliced

4 cups cider vinegar

½ cup olive oil

I cup mustard seeds (preferably white)

I tablespoon celery seeds

1. Wash the cucumbers well, and slice into ⅛-inch circles. Place in a large bowl, sprinkle with the salt, and allow to sit for 3 hours.

2. Drain the cucumbers of any accumulated juices, and pat dry with a paper towel. Return the cucumbers to the bowl.

3. Add the onions to the drained cucumber, and toss to combine.

4. Place the vinegar, olive oil, mustard seeds, and celery seeds in a large bowl, and stir to mix thoroughly.

5. Transfer the cucumber-onion mixture to two quart-sized sterilized jars, and ladle in the vinegar mixture, making sure that each jar receives a good number of seeds.

6. Store the pickles in the refrigerator for about 3 weeks before serving.

OLIVE AND GARBANZO BEAN TAPENADE

YIELD: ABOUT 2 CUPS

I can (8 ounces)
garbanzo beans,
rinsed and drained

1/2 cup chopped
black olives

1/4 cup minced
green olives

2 tablespoons minced
fresh coriander leaves

2 tablespoons fresh
lemon juice

I tablespoon olive oil

I clove roasted
garlic (page 162)

1/2 teaspoon paprika

1/8 teaspoon chili
powder

This delicious dish is a favorite in the Mideast.
If you like hummus, you'll love this exotic tapenade.

1. Place the drained garbanzo beans in a medium-sized bowl and mash lightly with a fork. Add all of the remaining ingredients and blend thoroughly.

2. Serve at room temperature with crisp crackers.

OLD-STYLE FRENCH TAPENADE

YIELD: ABOUT 2 CUPS

1/2 cup anchovies

I cup pitted
black olives

1/2 cup capers, rinsed
and drained

2 tablespoons
olive oil

This centuries-old tapenade—originally made by crushing the ingredients
with mortar and pestle—has been enjoyed in Provence since olives were
first harvested. It's so rich and delicious that some people call it
"Provençal caviar." You may use a mortar and pestle if you wish,
but a food processor is a whole lot faster.

1. Place the anchovies in a colander, and rinse to eliminate the excess salt. Pat dry with paper towels.

2. Place the anchovies, olives, and capers in a food processor or blender, and process until nicely puréed.

3. Add the olive oil to the olive mixture a little at a time, until the tapenade becomes smooth and creamy. If you prefer a looser consistency, add a little extra oil.

4. Serve at room temperature with warm crusty French bread.

CHUNKY HOT PEPPER DIP

Call this Mideast Salsa and you'll come close. It may be served hot from the pot, at room temperature, or cold. Provide something crisp for scooping and watch it disappear. This dip is also nice spooned into pita bread.

1. Place the olive oil in a large skillet over medium-low heat. When the oil is hot, add the bell peppers and cook, stirring occasionally, for 5 minutes, or until tender-crisp. Remove the peppers from the pan and set aside.

2. Add the tomatoes to the pan, sprinkle with the salt, and cook over high heat until the tomatoes begin to bubble. Reduce the heat to medium and cook, stirring occasionally, for 5 minutes.

3. Return the cooked peppers to the pan along with the garlic, jalapeño pepper, cumin, and paprika. Cook over medium heat, stirring occasionally, for about 5 minutes, or until the peppers are soft and the sauce has thickened. Stir in half of the cilantro, and continue cooking for 2 minutes.

4. Stir in the cayenne if desired, and taste and adjust the seasonings. Stir in the last half of the cilantro and serve hot, accompanied by crisp crackers.

YIELD: ABOUT
2 1/2 CUPS

1/4 cup olive oil

I green bell pepper, cut into 1/2-inch dice

I red bell pepper, cut into 1/2-inch dice

I yellow bell pepper, cut into 1/2-inch dice

I can (28 ounces) diced tomatoes, drained

2 teaspoons salt

3 cloves garlic, coarsely chopped

I jalapeño pepper, seeds and ribs removed, chopped

1/2 teaspoon ground cumin

1/2 teaspoon paprika

1/4 cup chopped fresh cilantro, divided

1/4 teaspoon cayenne pepper (optional)

YIELD: ABOUT 7 CUPS

MIXTURE ONE

2 cups canned pinto beans, rinsed and drained

1 cup grated Cheddar cheese

1 tablespoon minced onion

$1/2$ teaspoon salt

6 drops hot pepper sauce

2 tablespoons olive oil

MIXTURE TWO

2 ripe avocados, peeled and pitted

2 tablespoons lemon juice

$1/2$ teaspoon salt

Cracked pepper to taste

MIXTURE THREE

1 cup sour cream

$1/2$ cup mayonnaise

$1/2$ teaspoon dry taco seasoning mix

MIXTURE FOUR

1 jar (7 ounces) pitted black olives, drained and halved

3 ripe but firm tomatoes, coarsely diced

1 cup chopped scallions

EIGHT-LAYER MEXICAN DIP

This dish includes four different mixtures, but each delicious combination of ingredients is divided in half for assembly, so you'll end up with eight layers. My favorite layers are rich with luscious ripe olives.

1. To make Mixture One, place the beans in a medium-sized bowl and mash with a fork. Add all of the remaining ingredients except for the olive oil, and stir to combine.

2. Place the olive oil in a medium-sized skillet over medium heat. When the oil is hot, add the bean mixture and cook, stirring constantly, until the cheese is melted. Set aside.

3. To make Mixture Two, place all of the Mixture Two ingredients in a medium-sized bowl, and mash with a fork. Set aside.

4. To make Mixture Three, place all of the Mixture Three ingredients in a small bowl, and stir to combine. Set aside.

5. To make Mixture Four, place all of the Mixture Four ingredients in a large bowl, and stir to combine.

6. To assemble the dip, place half of Mixture One in a flat 9-x-9-inch glass dish, spreading evenly. Follow with half of Mixture Two, half of Mixture Three, and half of Mixture Four, spreading evenly in each case. Repeat the layers.

7. Serve immediately with crunchy tortilla chips.

SANDWICH SPREADS AND SANDWICHES

RIPE OLIVE AND CREAM CHEESE SPREAD

*The richness of ripe olives and the fresh, clean taste of crisp green pepper
make this spread a crowd pleaser.*

1. Place the cream cheese and cream or dressing in small bowl, and mix well with a fork.

2. Add all of the remaining ingredients to the cream cheese mixture, and combine well. Refrigerate until ready to use and enjoy on crackers or as a spread for open-faced sandwiches.

YIELD: 1 1/2 CUPS

I package (3 ounces) cream cheese, brought to room temperature

I tablespoon cream or any mild salad dressing

1/2 cup finely chopped black olives

1/2 cup finely minced green bell pepper

1/2 teaspoon salt

PECAN-OLIVE CREAM CHEESE SPREAD

*Crunchy pecans and salty olives are a winning combination.
The blue cheese adds still more tangy flavor, so by
all means use it if you like this ancient cheese.*

1. Place the cream cheese and cream in small bowl, and mix well with a fork.

2. Add all of the remaining ingredients to the cream cheese mixture, and combine well. Refrigerate until ready to use and enjoy on crackers or as a spread for open-faced sandwiches.

YIELD: 1 1/2 CUPS

I package (3 ounces) cream cheese, brought to room temperature

I tablespoon cream

1/2 cup chopped olives of your choice

1/2 cup chopped pecans

I tablespoon crumbled blue cheese (optional)

1/2 teaspoon salt

Making the Olive Oil Decision

As you leaf through the recipes in this chapter, you'll note that occasionally—when the type of olive oil is truly critical to success—I specify that the olive oil used should be extra virgin, light, or extra-light. In the majority of recipes, though, I do not indicate a specific type of oil. If you would like a little more guidance in making the olive oil decision, you've come to the right place.

Whenever olive oil is the star of the show, such as when you're making an infused oil to be drizzled on bread, it's best to use the finest quality oil available. In other words, it's wisest to use extra virgin olive oil. This will insure that you get the truest, richest olive taste—which is exactly what you want when you pour golden oil on a crusty loaf. When olive oil is used in salads, the taste also shines through, so you'll want to use either extra virgin or virgin. What about when olive oil is used for sautéing, as it is in so many recipes? As long as you're not deep-frying—a process that requires light olive oil, as it has a higher smoke point—feel free to use any grade of olive oil you have on hand. (For more information on the different grades of olive oils, see page 27 in Chapter 2.) In these recipes, the oil is usually used in relatively small amounts, and its flavor is less important than it is in an oil-and-vinegar-dressed salad, for instance.

If you're planning on making some infused olives oils (see page 130), you'll probably want to use these delightful creations in your cooking. If so, always take care to choose the one that will best enhance the other ingredients in the recipe. For example, a garlic-infused olive oil enhances roasted vegetables; a lemon-infused olive oil is perfect for making lemon chicken; and a herb-infused olive oil is a lovely foundation for home-made salad dressing. If you have none of these oils on hand, though, simply choose the best-quality olive oil that you have in your kitchen cupboard.

Finally, we come to baking. When making a savory bread that would be enhanced by rich olive flavor, choose extra virgin or virgin olive oil, as either one will give good results. But when making baked goods in which a distinctive olive taste is undesirable—Easy Devil's Food Cake is a good example—choose light or extra-light olive oil. With its lighter color and fragrance, this oil will add moistness to your baked goods without masking or competing with the flavors of key ingredients like chocolate and fruit.

OPEN-FACED MUSHROOM SANDWICH

YIELD: 8 SERVINGS

These crunchy delights can be turned into party fare by cutting each open-faced sandwich into triangles. Just be aware that they will go fast. Mushroom sandwiches are also quite wonderful served as a light supper or special luncheon; just add a green salad.

1. Place the mushrooms, oil, rosemary, and sage in a large saucepan. Stir to mix, cover, and cook over medium-high heat for about 8 minutes, stirring occasionally.

2. Uncover the saucepan and continue to cook, stirring often, for 15 to 20 minutes, or until most of the liquid has evaporated and the mushrooms are browned.

3. Stir the cornstarch into the broth, and add to the saucepan. Squeeze the garlic into the saucepan, and mix thoroughly. Cook over medium-high heat, stirring constantly, until the mixture comes to a boil and thickens.

4. Place the toasted bread slices on individual dinner plates, and top each with a liberal portion of the mushroom mixture and a sprinkling of Parmesan cheese. Enjoy immediately.

8 ounces each shiitake, chanterelle, and Portabella mushrooms, thinly sliced

2 tablespoons olive oil

I tablespoon each chopped fresh rosemary and sage, or I teaspoon each dried

2 teaspoons cornstarch

$^3/_4$ cup chicken or vegetable broth

I clove roasted garlic (see page 162)

8 thick slices sourdough bread, lightly toasted

2 tablespoons grated Parmesan cheese

YIELD: 4 SERVINGS

One 12–14-inch round loaf
of hearty bread

DRESSING

2 tablespoons olive oil

1 teaspoon apple cider
vinegar

½ teaspoon mustard

Salt and cracked pepper
to taste

2 scallions, minced

SPREAD

2 tablespoons olive oil

1 tablespoon lemon juice

1 clove roasted garlic
(see page 162)

1 tablespoon finely chopped
fresh basil

FILLING

2 cups coarsely slivered
salad greens

6 thin slices smoked ham

6–8 thin slices dry salami

6 thin slices provolone

4 ripe tomatoes, diced

1 cup coarsely chopped
black olives

THE ANTIPASTO SANDWICH

This sandwich is perfect for toting to a picnic or a pool party, and is also great while watching the big game. Set out bowls of crunchy tortilla chips and salsa, and let the party begin!

1. To prepare the bread, use a serrated knife to cut the loaf in half horizontally. Remove the center of the bread from both halves, leaving a 2-inch shell all around. Set aside.

2. To prepare the dressing, place all of the dressing ingredients except for the scallions in a small bowl, and whisk to combine. Stir in the scallions, and set aside.

3. To prepare the spread, place all of the spread ingredients in a food processor and pulse until the mixture is smooth. Alternatively, place the ingredients in a small bowl and whisk until well combined. Set aside.

4. To assemble the sandwich, cover the inside of each half of the loaf with the spread. Line the bottom half of the bread with half of the salad greens, and drizzle with half of the dressing.

5. Layer the meats, cheese, and tomatoes over the dressed greens, arranging them to fit. Sprinkle with the black olives, drizzle with the remaining dressing, and top with the remaining greens.

6. Fit the top of the loaf over the bottom, and wrap the loaf in aluminum foil. Place the loaf in the refrigerator, topping it with a plate weighed down to compress the ingredients. Chill for at least an hour or overnight, cut into fourths, and serve.

HEARTY VEGGIE SURPRISE SANDWICH

Although there's no meat in this recipe, it's not for vegetarians only. Meat- and veggie-lovers alike will love these crunchy treats, which are made even more flavorful with the addition of black olives.

1. To prepare the filling, place the tofu in a medium-sized bowl and mash with a fork. Add all of the remaining filling ingredients, and stir to combine well.

2. Pile the filling on the bottom half of the bread. Add the tomato, onion, bean sprouts, and lettuce, and pop on the second half of the bread. (If using pita bread, dice the tomato and onion and shred the lettuce before filling the pockets.) Serve immediately.

YIELD: 6 SERVINGS

6 servings bread of your choice, such as hearty wheat, split onion rolls, or pita bread

6 slices ripe beefsteak tomato

6 slices sweet red onion

I cup bean sprouts

6 leaves romaine or butter lettuce

FILLING

8 ounces tofu, drained

I cup shredded carrots

I cup fresh baby spinach

I cup sliced black olives

3 scallions with tops, minced

I tablespoon finely minced fresh basil

I clove garlic, minced

I tablespoon rice vinegar

I teaspoon fresh lemon juice

Salt and cracked pepper to taste

I package
(3 ounces) cream
cheese, brought to
room temperature

I tablespoon cream
or any mild salad
dressing

½ cup chopped
pimento-stuffed
green olives

¼ cup very finely
chopped celery

⅛ cup minced sweet
onion (optional)

¼ teaspoon salt

¼ teaspoon paprika

YIELD: 8½ OUNCES
INFUSED OLIVE OIL

2 cloves garlic,
slivered

8½-ounce bottle
extra virgin olive oil

STUFFED OLIVES AND CREAM CHEESE SPREAD

*The crunch of celery and onion beautifully complements the mellowness of
stuffed olives in this savory spread. Pimento bits add a welcome spark of color.*

1. Place the cream cheese and cream or dressing in small bowl, and mix
well with a fork.

2. Add all of the remaining ingredients to the cream cheese mixture, and
combine well. Refrigerate until ready to use and enjoy on crackers or
as a spread for open-faced sandwiches.

INFUSED OLIVE OILS

GARLIC-INFUSED OLIVE OIL

*This oil is a wonderful base for Italian salad dressing. Make it as garlicky
as you like by adjusting the amount of time the garlic remains in the oil.*

1. Drop the slivered garlic into the olive oil. Cap the bottle and let it rest
for 2 or 3 days.

2. Taste the oil, and if you like the result, remove the garlic. For a more
intense flavor, allow the garlic to remain in the oil.

LEMON-INFUSED OLIVE OIL

YIELD: 8 ½ OUNCES
INFUSED OLIVE OIL

I lemon

8 ½-ounce bottle
extra virgin olive oil

Use this oil to make a sweet and tangy citrus dressing for fruit.

1. Wash and dry the lemon. Using a vegetable peeler, sharp knife, or lemon zester, remove thin slivers of lemon zest all around the fruit. Be careful not to remove any of the white material on the inside of the peel, as it will impart a bitter flavor to the oil.

2. Drop the lemon zest into the oil, poking it down so that it remains immersed. Cap the bottle and let it rest for 1 week.

3. Taste the oil, and if you like the result, remove the peel. For a more intense flavor, allow the peel to remain in the oil.

A Dazzling Hostess Gift

Any of the infused oils in this chapter would make a welcome hostess gift—and a stunning one, as well, if you spend a little time on the presentation. Simply pour the finished oil into a decorative bottle, leaving in the herbs, sundried tomatoes, peppercorns, and other ingredients to provide visual interest. (Naturally, Garlic-and-Rosemary-Infused Olive Oil looks the most spectacular!) Cap the bottle, and tie several lengths of raffia around the top.

You can stop right there, if you wish, but to make a truly dazzling gift, wrap the oil in a checked napkin and nestle it in a basket, along with a loaf of crusty bread and a bottle of good Italian wine. Magnifico!

YIELD: 8 1/2 OUNCES
INFUSED OLIVE OIL

2 ounces
sundried tomatoes
(about 1/2 cup)

3 sprigs fresh thyme

8 1/2-ounce bottle
extra virgin olive oil

SUNDRIED TOMATO AND THYME OLIVE OIL

At our house, this is the bread spread of choice.
It really adds flavor to any sandwich.

1. To keep the oil from overflowing when other ingredients are added, pour about 3 ounces of the oil into another bottle or dish, and set aside.

2. Place the sundried tomatoes in a small heatproof bowl, and add boiling water to cover. Allow to sit for 10 minutes. Then drain off the water and pat the tomatoes dry with paper towels.

3. Drop the tomatoes and the thyme into the oil, poking the ingredients down so that they remain immersed. Add enough reserved oil to top off the bottle, add the cap, and let it rest for 1 week.

4. Taste the oil, and if you like the result, remove the tomatoes and thyme. For a more intense flavor, allow the ingredients to remain in the oil.

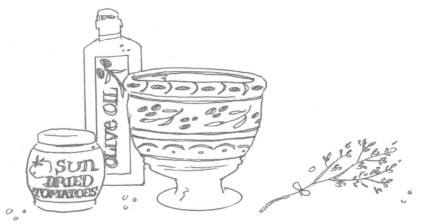

GARLIC-AND-ROSEMARY-INFUSED OLIVE OIL

YIELD: 14 OUNCES
INFUSED OLIVE OIL

I saved the best for last. This gourmet oil can be the basis for a delicious vinaigrette, but it's so good that you'll also enjoy it drizzled on crusty bread. The next time you're serving an Italian feast, simply provide good Italian bread and pass a cruet of infused olive oil for dipping and drizzling. You'll get raves.

17-ounce bottle
extra virgin olive oil

1 tablespoon
mustard seeds

$\frac{1}{2}$ tablespoon
peppercorns

$\frac{1}{2}$ clove garlic

Sprig fresh rosemary

1. To keep the oil from overflowing when other ingredients are added, pour about 3 ounces of the oil into another bottle or dish, and set aside.

2. Crack the mustard seeds and peppercorns, and drop them into the oil. Add the garlic.

3. Insert the sprig of fresh rosemary into the oil. If the sprig is too tall for the bottle, trim it to size.

4. Add enough reserved oil to top off the bottle, add the cap, and let it rest for 5 to 7 days.

5. Taste the oil, and if you like the result, remove the rosemary and garlic. The mustard seeds and peppercorns may remain, if you wish. For a more intense flavor, allow the rosemary and garlic to remain in the oil.

SALAD DRESSINGS AND SAUCES

THOMAS JEFFERSON'S FAVORITE DRESSING

YIELD: ABOUT
1½ CUPS

6 hard-boiled eggs

I teaspoon
prepared mustard

I teaspoon sugar

½ teaspoon salt

I cup olive oil

½ cup tarragon
vinegar

*If you read the inset on page 87, you know that Thomas Jefferson loved
olive oil. The following recipe was based on his favorite salad dressing.
Old "receipts" were most often prepared by eye and experience,
not by written rules, so there's no record of the measurements actually
used by Jefferson's staff. Through experimentation, though,
I've worked out amounts that I find pleasing. Feel free to make
further adjustments according to your own preferences.*

1. Cut the hard-boiled eggs in half, and separate the yolks from the
whites. Reserve the whites for future use, and transfer the egg yolks
to a small bowl. Mash the yolks lightly with a fork.

2. Add the mustard, sugar, and salt to the egg yolks, and stir to mix.

3. Place the olive oil in a medium-sized bowl, and whisk in the vinegar
and the egg yolk mixture.

4. Use immediately, or cover and refrigerate until ready to serve. If
desired, slice the reserved egg whites very thin and use them to garnish the salad, along with thinly sliced scallions.

CLASSIC VINAIGRETTE

YIELD: ABOUT $^3/_4$ CUP

All vinaigrettes start with olive oil and a form of acid—usually vinegar, but sometime lemon juice. I prefer vinegar because you can select from so many flavored varieties. Choose your favorite vinegar and the best olive oil you can find, and enjoy this classic dressing.

$^1/_2$ cup olive oil

3 tablespoons vinegar of your choice

1 teaspoon salt

Cracked pepper to taste

Dash cayenne pepper

1. Place the olive oil in a small bowl. Slowly add the vinegar, whisking constantly.

2. Add all of the remaining ingredients and whisk thoroughly.

3. Use the dressing immediately or transfer to a jar, pop on the top, and refrigerate. Bring to room temperature and shake thoroughly before serving.

TART AND SPICY VINAIGRETTE

YIELD: ABOUT 1 CUP

This piquant dressing is good on any crisp greens as well as on broccoli, and is wonderful with chicken.

$^1/_4$ cup fresh lemon juice

2 tablespoons grainy Dijon mustard

1 teaspoon sugar

$^1/_2$ cup olive oil

Salt and cracked pepper to taste

1. Place the lemon juice, mustard, and sugar in a small bowl, and whisk to combine.

2. Slowly drizzle in the olive oil, whisking constantly until thickened. Taste and adjust the seasonings, adding salt and pepper as needed.

3. Use the dressing immediately or transfer to a jar, pop on the top, and refrigerate. Bring to room temperature and shake thoroughly before serving.

YIELD: ABOUT 1 CUP

$^1/_2$ cup chopped
fresh cilantro

$^1/_4$ cup white wine
vinegar

I teaspoon Dijon
mustard

I shallot, minced

I clove garlic, minced

I green chile,
seeded and chopped

$^1/_4$ teaspoon salt

Cracked pepper

$^1/_2$ cup olive oil

SPICY VINAIGRETTE WITH CILANTRO

*This delicious dressing is a spicy surprise over mixed greens
and is excellent drizzled over roasted vegetables.
Try serving it with crab cakes, too.*

1. Place all of the ingredients except for the olive oil in a food processor
   or blender, and process until puréed.

2. Slowly add the olive oil to the mixture, blending until smooth.

3. Use the dressing immediately or transfer to a jar, pop on the top, and
   refrigerate. Bring to room temperature and shake thoroughly before
   serving.

YIELD: ABOUT 1 CUP

$^2/_3$ cup olive oil

$^1/_4$ cup unsweetened
apple juice

$2^1/_2$ tablespoons
orange, lemon, or
lime juice

$^1/_2$ clove garlic,
crushed (optional)

SWEET AND SASSY CITRUS VINAIGRETTE

*This vinaigrette is the perfect complement for a refreshing fruit salad. Use
whatever fresh fruits you prefer, arrange them artfully on a plate, and
drizzle on this delicious dressing. Then pass a basket of croissants and
a selection of muffins, and you have the ideal light lunch or supper.*

1. Place all of the ingredients in a small bowl, and whisk until smooth
   and thick.

2. Use the dressing immediately or transfer to a jar, pop on the top, and
   refrigerate. Bring to room temperature and shake thoroughly before
   serving.

ITALIAN DRESSING

YIELD: ABOUT $^3/_4$ CUP

For a quick Italian dressing, add the flavors of Italy to the Classic Vinaigrette blend presented on page 135. You probably have everything you need in your kitchen right now. This is the old-fashioned "real" Italian dressing, not the artificially thickened product you find in a bottle in the supermarket. It's also very good warmed and served over broccoli.

1 recipe Classic Vinaigrette (page 135)

2 tablespoons very finely minced green or red bell pepper

1 tablespoon very finely minced onion

$^1/_2$ clove garlic, finely minced

$^1/_2$ teaspoon sugar

$^1/_4$ teaspoon crumbled dried basil

$^1/_8$ teaspoon dried oregano

$^1/_8$ teaspoon celery salt

1. Place all of the ingredients in a jar. Cover and shake well to combine.

2. Refrigerate the dressing overnight, as this will allow the flavors to marry. This dressing gets better with time. Bring to room temperature and shake thoroughly before serving.

MAYONNAISE MUSTARD SAUCE

YIELD: $^1/_2$ CUP

This savory sauce is great on sandwiches, superb with cold meats, and truly spectacular over steamed cauliflower. Use either Mixer Mayo (see page 140) or a good store-bought brand.

$^1/_4$ cup mayonnaise

2 tablespoons Dijon mustard

2 tablespoons olive oil

1. Place all of the ingredients in a small bowl, and stir to mix thoroughly.

2. Use immediately or cover and refrigerate until ready to serve.

CLASSIC FRENCH DRESSING

¼ cup plus
2 tablespoons
olive oil, divided

2 tablespoons apple
cider vinegar, divided

I teaspoon sugar

¼ teaspoon salt

¼ teaspoon paprika

¼ teaspoon dry
mustard

I clove garlic
(optional)

Once upon a time, French dressing was a spicy clear dressing—not the thick, bright orange dressing you see today on supermarket shelves. This classic version is rich with flavor. I think you'll like it.

1. Place 1 tablespoon of the olive oil, 1 tablespoon of the vinegar, and all of the sugar, salt, paprika, and dry mustard in a small bowl, and whisk until smooth.

2. Add another 2 tablespoons of olive oil to the mixture, and whisk again until smooth.

3. Add all of the remaining olive oil and vinegar, and whisk well to combine.

4. Transfer the dressing to a jar, drop in the garlic if desired, and shake well. Use immediately, or refrigerate until ready to serve. Unless you really fancy garlic, remove it after a few days.
Bring to room temperature and shake thoroughly before serving.

TOMATO-SOUP FRENCH DRESSING

*This is the thick dressing we most often associate with
French Dressing today. Made with that old standby,
canned tomato soup, it's easy to prepare and quite flavorful.*

1. Place the tomato soup in a jar, and add the vinegar and olive oil. Use a narrow spatula or a spoon to stir the vinegar and oil into the soup.

2. Add all of the remaining ingredients to the jar, pop on the top, and shake well to blend.

3. Use the dressing immediately or refrigerate until ready to serve. Unless you really fancy garlic, remove it after a few days. Bring to room temperature and shake before serving.

YIELD: ABOUT 2 CUPS

1 can (10 1/2 ounces) condensed tomato soup

1 cup vinegar of your choice

1/2 cup olive oil

2 tablespoons sugar

1 tablespoon Worcestershire sauce

1 teaspoon dry mustard

1 teaspoon very finely minced onion

1/2 teaspoon paprika

1/2 teaspoon pepper

Salt to taste

1/2 clove garlic

OLIVE BUTTER

*If you are trying to replace some of the saturated fat in your diet
with a heart-healthy product, here's an easy and delicious way
to do it. Sublime on a baked potato, this spread will let you
"butter" your vegetables with a clear conscience.*

1. Place the butter and oil in a small bowl, and use an electric mixer set on low speed to blend thoroughly.

2. Spoon the spread into an airtight container and refrigerate until ready to serve. Note that this spread will be solid only when well chilled.

YIELD: 1 CUP

1/2 cup butter, softened

1/2 cup light olive oil

YIELD:
ABOUT 1¼ CUPS

I clove garlic,
halved lengthwise

¼ cup egg substitute

¼ cup ketchup

½ teaspoon
Worcestershire
sauce

½ teaspoon salt

¼ teaspoon dry
mustard

I cup olive oil

¼ cup vinegar of
your choice

MIXER MAYO

This is not your grandmother's mayonnaise; it's much easier to prepare.
Use your electric mixer, and the result will be a thick, velvety,
faintly pink, and definitely luscious mayonnaise.
Note that this mayo is made with egg substitute—a pasteurized
product that's just fine to use uncooked. Enjoy!

1. Rub the inside of a medium-sized bowl with the cut sides of the garlic. Be generous.

2. Place the egg substitute, ketchup, Worcestershire sauce, salt, and dry mustard in the prepared bowl, and use an electric mixer set on slow speed to beat until well combined.

3. Slowly add the olive oil to the egg mixture a few dribbles at a time, alternating with the vinegar. Increase the mixer speed in increments and beat until very thick. If the sauce is too thick, beat in a few drops of warm water until you have the consistency you like. Cover and refrigerate promptly, being sure to use within 1 week.

RÉMOULADE SAUCE

YIELD: ABOUT 1 CUP

This is the classic sauce that's so good served chilled with cold meats.
It's the new favorite with roasted vegetables, too,
and very elegant with crab cakes and other seafood.

1. Place the egg substitute, lemon juice, mustard, and salt in a food processor or blender, and pulse until well combined.

2. With the processor or blender still running, slowly drizzle in the oil until the mixture is smooth and thoroughly emulsified. Add all of the remaining ingredients and blend well.

3. Use immediately or cover and refrigerate until ready to serve.

$\frac{1}{4}$ cup egg substitute

2 tablespoons fresh lemon juice

I tablespoon prepared mustard

$\frac{1}{2}$ teaspoon salt

$\frac{1}{2}$ cup olive oil

$1\frac{1}{2}$ tablespoons chopped dill pickle

I tablespoon chopped fresh parsley

I tablespoon capers, rinsed and drained

$\frac{1}{2}$ tablespoon snipped fresh chives

I teaspoon tomato paste

SALADS

1 tablespoon apple cider vinegar

2 teaspoons sugar

3/4 cup sour cream

2 tablespoons olive oil

1 teaspoon celery seeds

3/4 teaspoon salt

Cracked pepper to taste

1 small head cabbage, finely shredded (3–4 cups)

CLASSIC COLE SLAW

If you're accustomed to deli cole slaw, try this classic recipe and discover how delicious cole slaw can be.

1. Place the vinegar in a small dish, and stir in the sugar until it dissolves. Set aside.

2. Place the sour cream in a medium-sized bowl, and stir in the olive oil until well blended.

3. Add the vinegar mixture to the sour cream mixture, and stir to combine. Add the celery seeds, salt, and pepper to taste, and stir to combine thoroughly.

4. Place the shredded cabbage in a large bowl, and add the dressing. Toss to mix thoroughly and serve immediately, or cover and refrigerate until ready to serve.

GREEK COLE SLAW

This Greek-style cole slaw differs from most American versions, as it doesn't contain sugar. But this recipe certainly doesn't skimp on flavor. You might think that the measurements are scant, but you'll find that the resulting dressing is more than sufficient to dress a small head of cabbage.

1. Place all of the ingredients except for the cabbage in a medium-sized bowl, and whisk together until smooth.

2. Place the shredded cabbage in a large bowl, and add the dressing. Toss to mix thoroughly and serve immediately, or cover and refrigerate until ready to serve.

YIELD: 4–6 SERVINGS

$1/3$ cup plain yogurt

3 tablespoons olive oil

1 small bunch dill, finely minced (about $1/2$ cup)

1 tablespoon red wine vinegar

1 tablespoon Dijon mustard

1 clove garlic, finely minced

Salt to taste

1 small head cabbage, finely shredded (3–4 cups)

YIELD: **4** SERVINGS

DRESSING

¼ cup white wine vinegar

2 teaspoons Dijon mustard

2 cloves garlic, crushed

Cracked pepper to taste

¾ cup olive oil

SALAD

I can (6 ounces) water-packed
Albacore tuna, drained and flaked

I pound fresh green beans,
cooked tender-crisp and chilled

6 small potatoes, preferably
new red, boiled, chilled,
and cut into bite-sized chunks

I cup canned artichoke hearts,
drained and quartered

½ cup pitted Niçoise or
black Kalamata olives

4 scallions, thinly sliced

8 ounces mixed salad greens
(3–4 cups)

GARNISH

4 ripe Roma tomatoes, quartered

2 hard-boiled eggs, quartered

I tablespoon capers,
rinsed and drained

4 anchovies (optional)

SALADE NIÇOISE

*This is the classic French recipe. One of my favorites,
it's hearty enough to be the mainstay of a meal—
served with flaky croissants, of course.*

1. Place all of the dressing ingredients except for the oil in a small bowl, and whisk until combined. Drizzle in the oil while whisking continually. Set aside.

2. Place all of the salad ingredients except for the mixed greens in a large bowl. Pour on a generous amount of dressing, and toss gently to coat. Cover and refrigerate for at least 2 hours.

3. To serve, dress the greens with the remaining dressing and divide equally among 4 plates. Mound the salad ingredients over the greens and garnish each salad with 4 tomato quarters, 2 egg quarters, a few capers, and an anchovy, if desired. Sprinkle a little extra cracked pepper over all and serve immediately.

OLIVE AND GARBANZO SALAD

YIELD: 4–6 SERVINGS

*This is another hearty salad that can be the backbone
of a luncheon or light supper. Serve with very good bread,
and pass some infused olive oil for drizzling or dipping.*

1. Place all of the dressing ingredients in a food processor or blender, and pulse until well combined. Alternatively, place the ingredients in a small bowl, and whisk until well mixed.

2. Place all of the salad ingredients in a large bowl, and toss to combine. Drizzle on the dressing and toss to coat.

3. Divide the salad among 4 to 6 chilled salad bowls. Sprinkle a little Parmesan over each serving, top with a portion of the croutons, and serve immediately.

DRESSING

1 tablespoon plus
1 teaspoon fresh
lemon juice

1 tablespoon honey

2 teaspoons olive oil

2 teaspoons Dijon
mustard

2 cloves garlic,
crushed

SALAD

2 cans (15 ounces
each) garbanzo
beans (chickpeas),
rinsed and drained

1 cup pitted
black olives

1/4 cup finely
chopped fresh basil

3 tablespoons
capers, rinsed
and drained

GARNISH

3 tablespoons
grated Parmesan
cheese

1 cup croutons

YIELD: 4–6 SERVINGS

DRESSING

3 tablespoons
olive oil

Juice of 1 lemon

SALAD

4 ounces sundried
tomatoes

1/3 cup golden raisins

1 can (15 ounces)
garbanzo beans
(chickpeas), rinsed
and drained

1/3 cup halved
black olives

GARNISH

1/3 cup coarsely
chopped walnuts

1/3 cup crumbled
feta cheese

GREEK-INSPIRED GARBANZO PICNIC SALAD

*This inspired combination is a good traveler. There's no mayonnaise
to worry about, so you can take it along on a picnic.
It's also a welcome addition to the buffet table.
It even makes a great light meal!*

1. Place the sundried tomatoes and raisins in a small heatproof bowl, and add boiling water to cover. Allow to sit for 10 minutes. Then drain off the water and pat dry with paper towels.

2. Using kitchen scissors or a small knife, cut the sundried tomatoes into slivers.

3. Transfer the tomatoes and raisins to a large bowl, and add the garbanzo beans and olives. Toss to combine.

4. Drizzle the olive oil and lemon juice over the bean mixture, and toss to coat. Cover and set aside at room temperature for 30 minutes to allow the flavors to meld.

5. Divide the salad among 4 to 6 salad bowls, sprinkle evenly with the walnuts and feta cheese, and serve immediately.

TABBOULEH

YIELD: **4–6** SERVINGS

*Appreciated throughout the Mideast, this grain salad
makes a great side dish or a light change-of-pace entrée.*

1. Place the bulghur wheat in large bowl and cover with cold water. Allow it to soak for about 3 hours, adding water as needed to keep the wheat covered. The wheat should be soft, but still a little chewy.

2. Drain the bulghur thoroughly, and return it to the bowl. Add the remaining ingredients, and stir to mix.

3. Refrigerate for 1 hour, or until completely chilled, and serve with crisp crackers or pita bread.

8 ounces medium-grind bulghur wheat (2 cups)

3 medium plum tomatoes, chopped

2 medium scallions, light green and white parts only, coarsely chopped

I tablespoon chopped fresh mint

I tablespoon vinegar of your choice

I tablespoon olive oil

YIELD: **4** SERVINGS

DRESSING

3 tablespoons
olive oil

3 tablespoons red
wine vinegar

2 teaspoons sugar

SALAD

1 medium-sized
eggplant

1 pound firm ripe
tomatoes, such as
Roma or plum

8 scallions, chopped,
green stems
included

1/3 cup halved or
quartered olives
of your choice

1/4 cup capers, rinsed
and drained

2 cloves garlic,
finely minced

GARNISH

1/4 cup pine nuts

1/4 cup chopped
fresh basil

ITALIAN ANTIPASTO SALAD

*Whether you serve this salad as a side dish or as part of an
antipasto tray, expect compliments. Tangy and delicious,
it's hearty enough to qualify as a light meal.*

1. Peel the eggplant and dice it into 1/2-inch pieces. To cook, place the
eggplant in a microwave-safe bowl. Add 1 tablespoon of water, cover
with plastic wrap, and cook on high for 6 to 7 minutes, or until tender. Alternatively, place the eggplant in a saucepan, cover with water,
and simmer for 10 to 12 minutes, or until tender. Set aside and allow
to cool.

2. Transfer the cooled eggplant to a large bowl. Add the tomatoes, scallions, olives, capers, and garlic, and toss to mix.

3. Place all of the dressing ingredients in a small bowl, and whisk
together to mix. Pour the dressing over the vegetables and toss gently
to mix. For full flavor, set aside for at least 30 minutes.

4. To toast the pine nuts, place the nuts in a small skillet that has been
preheated over medium-high heat. Heat, shaking the pan to keep the
nuts moving, until the nuts turn golden in color. Remove from the
pan and allow to cool.

5. To serve, divide the salad among 4 plates. Sprinkle with the chopped
basil and pine nuts, and serve immediately.

ISLAND VEGETABLE SALAD

Deliciously different, this inspired combination of ingredients hints as much of steamy bazaars as it does of island breezes.

1. Place all of the salad ingredients except for the lettuce in a large bowl, and toss gently to combine.

2. Place all of the dressing ingredients in a small bowl, and whisk together to mix. Pour the dressing over the salad ingredients and toss gently to mix.

3. To serve, divide the lettuce among 4 plates. Arrange the dressed salad over the lettuce, and serve immediately.

YIELD: 4 SERVINGS

DRESSING

$\frac{1}{2}$ cup coconut milk

1 tablespoon lemon juice

1 clove garlic, finely minced

$\frac{1}{2}$ teaspoon ground cumin

$\frac{1}{2}$ teaspoon dried basil

$\frac{1}{8}$ teaspoon ground turmeric

SALAD

2 cups canned garbanzo beans (chickpeas), rinsed and drained

1 cup halved cherry tomatoes

1 cup halved black olives

$\frac{1}{2}$ cup diced shallots

$\frac{1}{2}$ cup thinly sliced mushrooms

$\frac{1}{2}$ green bell pepper, cut into bite-sized chunks

$\frac{1}{2}$ red bell pepper, cut into bite-sized chunks

$\frac{1}{2}$ head iceberg lettuce, torn into bite-sized pieces

YIELD: 6 SERVINGS

DRESSING

¼ cup raspberry vinegar

8 leaves fresh basil, julienned

½ teaspoon dried tarragon

¼ teaspoon salt

½ cup olive oil

2 tablespoons cream

SALAD

1 head butter lettuce

1 unpeeled small seedless cucumber, cut in half and thinly sliced

18 ripe strawberries, quartered

½ small red onion, cut in half and thinly sliced

½ cup sliced almonds

Cracked pepper to taste

STRAWBERRY AND RED ONION SUMMER SALAD

My very good friend Shirley introduced me to this truly delicious dish several years ago. I made a face when she said "strawberries and onions," but changed my mind after one bite. You'll love it.

1. Place all of the dressing ingredients except for the oil and cream in a food processor or blender, and process until well mixed. With the processor still going, drizzle in the olive oil and process until emulsified. Add the cream. Transfer to a covered dish and refrigerate for at least 2 hours to blend the flavors. Overnight storage is even better.

2. To serve, divide the lettuce among 6 plates. Arrange all of the other salad ingredients over the lettuce, and drizzle with the dressing just before serving.

GRILLED SHRIMP SURPRISE SALAD

You've never had shrimp this delicious. The inspired marinade and delectable dressing make all the difference.

1. To prepare the marinade, place all of the marinade ingredients in a small bowl, and stir to combine. Transfer the shrimp to the marinade, cover, and set aside for at least 30 minutes.

2. While the shrimp are marinating, prepare the dressing by placing the first 9 dressing ingredients in a food processor or blender, and processing until smooth. Add the remaining dressing ingredients, and process to mix. Set aside at room temperature.

3. Preheat an outdoor barbecue grill or oven broiler. Remove the shrimp, discarding the marinade, and thread the shrimp onto skewers. Place the shrimp on the heated grill or under the broiler, about 4 to 5 inches from the heat source, and cook for 2 to 3 minutes on each side, or until the shrimp turn pink. Do not overcook.

4. To serve, divide the mixed greens among 4 plates, and drizzle with the dressing. Arrange 5 shrimp on each plate, and pass the extra dressing around the table.

YIELD: 4 SERVINGS

20 uncooked large shrimp, peeled and deveined

1 ½ cups mixed baby greens

MARINADE

½ cup dry sherry

½ cup soy sauce

¼ cup olive oil

¼ cup brown sugar

2 teaspoons minced garlic

3 slices fresh ginger root, crushed to release juices

Cracked pepper to taste

DRESSING

1 cup olive oil

⅓ cup peanut butter

1 small onion, cut into slivers

3 tablespoons minced fresh ginger root

2 teaspoons sugar

1 teaspoon salt

½ stalk celery, finely sliced

¼ teaspoon hot pepper sauce

Cracked pepper to taste

½ cup soy sauce

½ cup fresh lemon juice

¼ cup white wine vinegar

ARABIAN OLIVE, ONION, AND ORANGE SALAD

YIELD: **4** SERVINGS

4 large oranges, peeled and cut into small pieces

I small onion, thinly sliced and separated into rings

$1/2$ cup halved black olives

I tablespoon olive oil

I teaspoon fresh lemon juice

4 lettuce cups (single curved leaves)

*This refreshing combination of ingredients is good any time.
Chances are, you already have everything you
need in your kitchen.*

1. Place the oranges, onion, and olives in a medium-sized bowl, and toss to mix.

2. Drizzle the olive oil and lemon juice over the orange mixture, and toss gently.

3. Divide the salad evenly among the 4 lettuce cups. This salad is most flavorful at room temperature, so serve immediately.

SUNNY MEDITERRANEAN OLIVE AND ORANGE SALAD

YIELD: **4** SERVINGS

4 large oranges, peeled and cut into small pieces

$1/2$ cup halved black olives

$1/2$ teaspoon ground cumin

$1/8$ teaspoon cayenne pepper

4 lettuce cups (single curved leaves)

*This combination from the sunny Mediterranean makes a
truly delicious salad. Quickly and easily prepared, it will
also be quickly eaten because every bite is a delight.*

1. Place the oranges and olives in a medium-sized bowl, and toss to mix. Refrigerate for at least 1 hour, or until ready to serve.

2. Just before serving, mix the cumin and cayenne together in a small dish.

3. Divide the orange and olive mixture evenly among the 4 lettuce cups. Sprinkle the spice mixture evenly over each, and serve immediately.

GREEK GREEN BEAN SALAD

*Toss this hearty salad together, set out some crusty bread
and a big bowlful of marinated olives, and call it lunch.*

1. Wash the beans and snip off the ends. Snap in two, if desired. Steam over boiling water for 10 to 12 minutes, or just until tender-crisp. Rinse under cold water, drain, and set aside.

2. To toast the pine nuts, place them in a small skillet that has been pre-heated over medium-high heat. Heat, shaking the pan to keep the nuts moving, until the nuts turn golden in color. Remove from the pan and allow to cool.

3. Place the steamed beans, pine nuts, tomato chunks, garlic, and mint in a large bowl, and toss to mix. Drizzle with the olive oil and vinegar, add salt and cracked pepper to taste, and toss again.

4. Cover the salad and refrigerate for 1 hour before serving.

1 pound fresh green beans

3 tablespoons pine nuts

2 large ripe tomatoes, cut into bite-sized chunks

2 cloves garlic, minced

1 small bunch fresh mint leaves, shredded

¼ cup olive oil

2 tablespoons red wine vinegar

Salt and cracked pepper to taste

YIELD: **4** SERVINGS

DRESSING

2½ tablespoons olive oil

1 tablespoon soy sauce

¼ teaspoon sugar

¼ teaspoon ground ginger

⅛ teaspoon crushed garlic

SALAD

1 cup cooked rice, chilled

⅓ cup halved olives
of your choice

⅓ cup thinly sliced
mushrooms

⅓ cup thinly sliced scallions

⅓ cup bean sprouts

¼ cup chunks green
bell pepper

¼ cup chunks red
bell pepper

GARNISH

⅓ cup cashew pieces

CHINESE RICE SALAD

*You'll recognize the Chinese influence in this rice salad.
There's a hint of garlic and ginger, plus soy sauce,
of course—the "big three" of Chinese cooking.*

1. Place all of the salad ingredients in a large bowl, and toss to mix.

2. Place the oil in a small bowl, and whisk in the other dressing ingredients until well mixed.

3. Drizzle the dressing over the salad mixture and toss to combine. Sprinkle the cashews over all, and serve immediately.

CLASSIC ITALIAN BREAD SALAD

Yes, bread. Not croutons. In Tuscany, they call this Panzanella.
It's different and delicious. This salad cries out for very good
country-style bread. Don't try making it with anything less.
Best served at room temperature, this is an interesting addition
to a patio party or picnic, and a wonderful surprise on a buffet table.

1. Dip the bread briefly in cold water, 1 slice at a time. Squeeze out the water, tear the bread into pieces, and place in a medium-sized bowl.

2. Add all of the remaining salad ingredients to the bread, and toss gently to mix.

3. Place the dressing ingredients in a small bowl, and whisk until well mixed.

4. Drizzle the dressing over the salad mixture, toss to combine, and serve immediately.

YIELD: 4 SERVINGS

DRESSING

1/3 cup olive oil

1/3 cup balsamic vinegar

SALAD

8 thick slices stale country-style bread

8 firm ripe tomatoes, such as Roma or plum, coarsely chopped

2 unpeeled seedless cucumbers, coarsely chopped

8 scallions, sliced

1/2 cup slivered fresh basil

Salt and cracked pepper to taste

YIELD: **8** SERVINGS

I cup mayonnaise

¹/₄ cup finely chopped onion

¹/₂ cup sliced olives of your choice

¹/₂ tablespoon prepared mustard

8 small red potatoes (about I ¹/₂ pounds), cooked, peeled, cubed, and cooled

Salt and cracked pepper to taste

I pound American cheese, cubed

8 ounces bacon, cooked, drained, and crumbled

ALL-AMERICAN HOT POTATO SALAD

Featuring bacon, cheese, and, of course, olives, this hearty salad is a winner. I have a friend who is always asked to bring this to church potluck dinners and neighborhood patio parties. However, because it calls for mayonnaise, don't plan on taking it outside your own backyard unless you know what time the food will be served.

1. Place the mayonnaise in a large bowl. Add the onion, olives, and mustard, and stir until well mixed.

2. Add the cubed potatoes to the mayonnaise mixture. Sprinkle lightly with salt and cracked pepper, and use a large spoon to gently incorporate the potatoes into the mayonnaise.

3. Add the cheese cubes, and stir again to mix well.

4. Lightly grease a 9-x-11-inch baking dish with olive oil cooking spray, and turn the potato salad into the dish. Sprinkle the crumbled bacon over the top and bake uncovered in a preheated 300°F oven for 30 to 40 minutes, or until the cheese is melted and bubbling. Serve immediately.

ITALIAN-FLAG DILLED VEGETABLES

YIELD: 6–8 SERVINGS

This salad of marinated vegetables incorporates the colors of the Italian flag—red, green, and white. Nicely tart, and utterly delicious.

1. Cook the frozen cauliflower and broccoli according to package directions. Let cool and cut into bite-sized pieces.

2. Place all of the marinade ingredients in a medium-sized bowl, and whisk together to mix.

3. Add the cauliflower, broccoli, and slivered red pepper to the marinade, and toss to coat well. Serve immediately or cover and refrigerate until needed, bringing to room temperature before serving.

8 ounces frozen cauliflower florets

8 ounces frozen broccoli florets

$1/4$ cup slivered red bell pepper

MARINADE

$1/3$ cup olive oil

$1/4$ cup vinegar

I clove garlic, crushed, or $1/2$ teaspoon garlic powder

I tablespoon chopped fresh dill, or $1/2$ teaspoon dried dill

I teaspoon prepared mustard

I teaspoon sugar

Salt and cracked pepper to taste

SOUPS

GREEK VEGETABLE SOUP

YIELD: 6–8 SERVINGS

I cup olive oil, divided

3 onions, diced

3 large carrots, peeled and thinly sliced

2 stalks celery, thinly sliced

2 large potatoes, peeled and cut into small dice

4 large tomatoes, peeled, seeded, and chopped

I bunch flat-leaf parsley, finely chopped

8 cups water

8 ounces fresh spinach, washed and shredded

2 tablespoons fresh lemon juice

Salt and cracked pepper to taste

Grated Parmesan cheese (optional)

This heart-healthy soup calls for no meat. Even if you're not a vegetarian, you'll find it wonderfully hearty. Add a crisp salad and some crunchy bread, and you have a satisfying meal.

1. Place ½ cup of the olive oil in a large pot over medium heat. When the oil is hot, add the onions and cook, stirring occasionally, for about 7 minutes, or until translucent but not brown.

2. Add the carrots and celery to the pot, stir to coat with the oil, and sauté for 5 minutes, stirring often.

3. Add the potatoes, and stir to coat with the oil. Stir in the tomatoes, parsley, and water.

4. Increase the heat to bring the mixture to a boil. Reduce the heat and simmer uncovered for 30 minutes.

5. Add the spinach to the pot, and simmer for another 20 minutes. Add the lemon juice and salt and pepper to taste.

6. Just before serving, stir in the remaining ½ cup of olive oil. Ladle the soup into large bowls and float a few teaspoons of Parmesan cheese on top, if desired. Serve with chunks of crusty bread.

HEARTY BEAN SOUP

*Here's a robust vegetarian delight that's so good, you won't miss the meat.
This is another soup that should be served with a crisp green salad
and excellent bread.*

1. Place $\frac{1}{2}$ cup of the olive oil in a large pot over medium heat. When the oil is hot, add the onions and cook, stirring occasionally, for about 7 minutes, or until translucent but not brown.

2. Add the carrots, celery, and garlic to the pot, stir to coat with the oil, and cook for about 5 minutes, or until soft, stirring often.

3. Add the beans to the pot, and stir to coat with the oil. Stir in the water, tomatoes, and hot pepper.

4. Increase the heat to bring the mixture to a boil. Reduce the heat, and simmer uncovered for $1\frac{1}{2}$ to 2 hours, or until the beans are very tender.

5. Add salt and pepper to taste. Stir in the vinegar and the remaining $\frac{1}{2}$ cup of olive oil.

6. Ladle the soup into large bowls and serve with a basket of hearty bread.

YIELD: 6–8 SERVINGS

1 cup olive oil, divided

2 large onions, halved lengthwise and thinly sliced

2 carrots, peeled and thinly sliced

2 stalks celery, thinly sliced

2 cloves garlic, slivered

8 ounces small white beans, such as Great Northern, soaked overnight according to package directions, and drained

8 cups water

6 plum tomatoes, peeled, seeded, and chopped

1 fresh hot pepper, thinly sliced (optional)

Salt and cracked pepper to taste

2–3 tablespoons red wine vinegar

FISHERMAN'S SOUP

¾ cup olive oil, divided

3 large onions, thinly sliced

6 ripe plum tomatoes, peeled, seeded, and chopped

6 cups water

3 pounds firm white fish, such as halibut or cod, cut into large chunks

1 pound uncooked shrimp, peeled and deveined

2 large potatoes, peeled and cut into chunks

Salt and cracked pepper to taste

¼ cup finely chopped flat-leaf parsley

6–8 thick slices crusty bread, toasted

This thick and hearty seafood soup makes a satisfying entrée on a cold winter's night.

1. Place ½ cup of the olive oil in a large pot over medium heat. When the oil is hot, add the onions and cook, stirring occasionally, for about 7 minutes, or until translucent but not browned.

2. Add the tomatoes and water to the pot, and increase the heat to bring the mixture to a boil. Reduce the heat and allow the soup to simmer uncovered for 15 minutes. Remove the vegetables with a slotted spoon, and set aside.

3. Add the fish and shrimp to the pot, and simmer for 20 minutes. Return the vegetables to the pot, and add the potatoes. With the lid slightly ajar to allow steam to escape, simmer for 2 hours, or until very thick, stirring occasionally and adding more water if necessary.

4. Just before serving, add salt and pepper to taste, and stir in the parsley and the remaining olive oil.

5. Place 1 slice of bread in the bottom of each of the soup bowls. Ladle on the steaming soup and serve immediately.

GAZPACHO

YIELD: **6** SERVINGS

If you're not acquainted with gazpacho—a chilled vegetable soup—let me be the first to introduce it to you. This healthy, delicious, low-cal soup originated in Spain, and is one of my favorite "diet delights." Enjoy as a first course, or serve it with good bread and call it lunch. Pass some infused olive oil for drizzling on the bread, and expect raves.

1. Place the vegetables and cilantro in a food processor or blender, and process until coarsely chopped while slowly adding the olive oil and vinegar. Don't overprocess, but leave slightly chunky. You don't want a purée. Alternatively, cut the vegetables into a small dice, chop the cilantro, and combine with the oil and vinegar.

2. Add the thyme and salt and pepper to taste, and transfer the gazpacho to a covered container. Chill for at least 8 hours or overnight, and serve very cold.

7 ripe plum tomatoes

2 green or red bell peppers

2 small seedless cucumbers, peeled

1/2 sweet onion

2 cloves garlic

1 small bunch fresh cilantro

1/2 cup olive oil

2 tablespoons red wine vinegar

3/4 teaspoon dried thyme

Salt and cracked pepper to taste

VEGETABLES

READY-WHEN-YOU-ARE ROASTED GARLIC

YIELD: 1 HEAD
ROASTED GARLIC

1 head garlic

1 tablespoon
olive oil

Roasting garlic is both easy and rewarding. Roasting tames garlic, making the flavor rich and deep, and eliminating all sharpness and bitterness. Those little clay dishes designed to roast garlic are nice, but if you don't have one (and I don't), you'll find that a square of foil works beautifully.

1. Prepare the head of garlic by cutting a slice off the top. Be sure to shear a bit off the top of each individual clove so that all are exposed.

2. Place the garlic cut-side up in the middle of a square of aluminum foil, and drizzle with the olive oil. Then bring the 4 corners of the foil together at the top, and twist to completely enclose the garlic.

3. Place the garlic directly on the oven rack of a preheated 275°F oven, and roast for 45 minutes to an hour, or until soft to the touch when gently squeezed. Remove the garlic from the oven and allow it to cool.

4. To use immediately, just turn the head of garlic upside down and squeeze. The individual cloves will pop right out. Spread the garlic on crusty bread, or use in any recipe calling for garlic. To store, squeeze the cloves into a very small container, cover with a little olive oil, and snap on the cover. Your roasted garlic will be ready when you are, and it will wait indefinitely. Whenever you use the garlic—or the oil, which will quickly become infused with the garlic flavor—top it off with enough olive oil to cover. Do not refrigerate.

ROASTED MIXED VEGETABLES

Roasted vegetables are uniquely delicious and are an excellent
accompaniment to any entrée. Serve the vegetables hot out of the
oven, or chill them and serve them cold on an antipasto platter.
Although a combination of vegetables has been suggested,
feel free to add and subtract according to your preferences.

1. Scrub all vegetables and cut into bite-sized pieces.

2. Place the olive oil and garlic in a large bowl, and stir to mix. Add the vegetables, and toss to coat.

3. Arrange the vegetables in a single layer on a shallow baking pan, and lightly sprinkle with salt and cracked pepper to taste. Place in a preheated 400°F oven and roast, stirring occasionally, for 35 to 45 minutes, or until tender.

4. Sprinkle the roasted vegetables with the oregano, basil, and cheese, and either serve immediately or chill for later use.

YIELD: 6–8 SERVINGS

2 beets, peeled

1 small eggplant, unpeeled

2 new red potatoes, unpeeled

1 yam, peeled

1 green bell pepper, cut in half and flattened with the palm of your hand

1 red bell pepper, cut in half and flattened with the palm of your hand

6 baby carrots

1 onion

6 firm tomatoes, such as Roma or plum

4–6 tablespoons olive oil

2 cloves garlic, minced

Salt and cracked pepper to taste

2 teaspoons dried oregano

2 teaspoons dried basil

¼ cup grated Parmesan cheese

YIELD: **4–6** SERVINGS

6–8 red bell or jalapeño peppers, cut in half and flattened with the palm of your hand

2 tablespoons olive oil

MARINADE

1/3 cup olive oil

1/3 cup balsamic vinegar or red wine vinegar

10 leaves fresh basil, slivered, or 1 teaspoon dried basil

2 cloves garlic, finely minced

ROASTED PEPPERS IN MARINADE

Roasted peppers glistening with a flavorful marinade are a delicious addition to any sandwich, or just perched atop a piece of garlic toast that's been drizzled with olive oil. They go fast as part of an antipasto platter, and are wonderful in salads, too. Use this recipe with sweet bell peppers or jalapeños—whichever you prefer.

1. Place the peppers and olive oil in a large bowl, and toss to coat.

2. Arrange the peppers in a single layer on a shallow baking pan, and roast in a preheated 400°F oven, stirring occasionally, for 35 to 45 minutes, or until tender. Set aside to cool.

3. Place all of the marinade ingredients in a small bowl, and whisk until well combined.

4. Cut the roasted peppers into wide strips, and arrange the strips in a shallow bowl. Pour the marinade over the peppers and refrigerate overnight to allow all the flavors to meld.

5. Serve the peppers as desired, storing any leftovers in the refrigerator for up to a week.

ROASTED PORTABELLA MUSHROOMS

YIELD: **4–6** SERVINGS

*An ideal accompaniment to any meal, roasted mushrooms are especially
good with steak. This might look like a lot of mushrooms when
you're filling the baking dish, but remember that
mushrooms reduce in size as they cook.*

I pound Portabella
mushrooms, cut into
thick slices

I tablespoon
olive oil

I tablespoon
chopped fresh basil

1. Coat an 8-x-8-inch baking dish with olive oil cooking spray. Arrange
the mushrooms in the dish, and sprinkle with the olive oil and basil.
Toss gently to coat, and cover with aluminum foil.

2. Bake in a preheated 350°F oven for about 10 minutes, or until the
mushrooms are tender. Serve hot.

OLIVE OIL-ROASTED POTATOES

YIELD: **4–6** SERVINGS

*If your family wants potatoes with every meal, here's an easy way
to prepare them. Simple to put together, this dish requires
little attention once you've popped it in the oven.*

3 large baking
potatoes, such as
russets

2 tablespoons
olive oil

1. Peel the potatoes and cut them into chunks. Place them in a large
bowl, drizzle with the olive oil, and toss to coat.

2. Arrange the potatoes in a single layer on a shallow baking pan, and
bake in a preheated 350°F oven for about 50 minutes, or until the
potatoes are easily pierced with a fork. Serve hot.

OVEN-ROASTED DIRTY POTATOES

YIELD: 4–6 SERVINGS

3 large baking potatoes, such as russets

2 tablespoons olive oil

I teaspoon chopped fresh parsley

½ teaspoon paprika

½ teaspoon garlic powder

⅛ teaspoon black pepper

These potatoes are similar to Olive Oil-Roasted Potatoes (see page 165), except for the seasoning, which makes them special enough for company. Fix them in advance and slide them into the oven about 30 minutes before serving.

1. Scrub the potatoes, but do not peel them. Cut into ½-inch slices.

2. Place the potatoes and all of the remaining ingredients in a large plastic bag, seal, and shake until the slices are well coated.

3. Arrange the potatoes in a single layer on a shallow baking pan, and bake in a preheated 425°F oven for about 15 minutes, or until browned. Turn the slices and bake for another 15 minutes, or until the second side is browned. Serve hot.

BABY LIMA BEANS WITH GARLIC AND TARRAGON

YIELD: 4 SERVINGS

I package (I pound) frozen baby lima beans

I tablespoon olive oil

I clove garlic, finely minced

I tablespoon chopped fresh tarragon, or I teaspoon dried tarragon

If you don't like lima beans, this recipe may change your mind. It's quick and easy and awfully good.

1. Cook the baby limas as directed on the package, and drain well. Transfer the beans to a serving bowl.

2. Drizzle the olive oil over the beans, and sprinkle with the garlic and tarragon. Toss to coat and serve immediately.

ROASTED GREEN BEANS

This inspired dish lifts green beans above the mundane.
Your family will love Roasted Green Beans,
and they're special enough to serve to company with pride.

1. Wash the beans and snip off the ends. Pat dry.

2. Place the olive oil, garlic, oregano, salt, and pepper in a large bowl, and stir to mix. Add the beans and toss to coat.

3. Arrange the beans in a single layer on a shallow baking pan, and bake in a preheated 400°F oven for 10 minutes. Stir, sprinkle with the lemon juice, and return to the oven for an additional 10 minutes, or until the beans are tender-crisp when pierced with the tip of a knife.

4. While the beans are roasting, prepare the topping by combining the crumbs, olive oil, and garlic salt in a small bowl. Sprinkle the crumbs over the top of the cooked beans, add a sprinkling of cheese if desired, and serve immediately.

YIELD: 4–6 SERVINGS

1 pound fresh green beans

1 tablespoon olive oil

1 clove garlic, minced

1 teaspoon crushed dried oregano

1 teaspoon salt

Cracked pepper to taste

Juice of $\frac{1}{2}$ lemon

TOPPING

$\frac{1}{4}$ cup unflavored bread crumbs

1 teaspoon olive oil

$\frac{1}{8}$ teaspoon garlic salt

2–3 tablespoons shaved Romano cheese (optional)

ENTREES

MEDITERRANEAN VEGETABLE BAKE

This unusual vegetarian casserole is not only delectable as a light supper,
but is also the perfect accompaniment to your favorite meat dish.

YIELD: 4 SERVINGS

¼ cup olive oil

2 sweet onions,
cut in half and
thinly sliced

½ green bell pepper,
slivered

½ red bell pepper,
slivered

4 unpeeled zucchini,
halved lengthwise
and thinly sliced

I teaspoon
dried basil

Salt and cracked
pepper to taste

⅛ cup flour

4 firm tomatoes,
diced

I cup pitted
black olives

½ cup pine nuts

¼ cup balsamic
vinegar

⅓ cup slivered
fresh basil

1. Place the oil in a large skillet over medium heat. When the oil is hot, add the onions and peppers and sauté for about 5 minutes, or until tender. Stir in the zucchini and sauté for an additional 2 minutes, or until the zucchini is tender. Stir in the dried basil and add salt and cracked pepper to taste.

2. Arrange the vegetables in a shallow 8-x-8-inch baking dish. Sprinkle evenly with the flour and spread the diced tomatoes over the top.

3. Bake, uncovered, in a preheated 300°F oven for 20 minutes. Distribute the olives and pine nuts evenly over the top, and return the casserole to the oven for 10 minutes to warm the olives. Drizzle the vinegar evenly over all, sprinkle with the basil, and serve immediately.

PENNE PASTA AND OLIVES WITH ORANGE ZEST

YIELD: 4–6 SERVINGS

This Greek treat marries the mellow richness of olives with the sweet-tart taste of orange zest. If you've eaten pasta abroad, you know that it's traditional to toss the sauce with the pasta, resulting in the flavor of the sauce being all but lost. However, I've chosen to place the sauce on top so that you can taste and enjoy every drop.

2 tablespoons salt

2 unpeeled medium zucchini, coarsely diced

1 pound penne pasta

Olive oil

1 1/2 cups pitted Kalamata olives or other black olives

4 ripe plum tomatoes, coarsely chopped

1/4 cup snipped fresh rosemary

2 cloves garlic, finely minced

GARNISH

1/2 cup pine nuts

1/2 cup crumbled feta cheese

Zest of 1 orange

1. Fill a large pot with water, and stir in the salt. Bring the pot to a boil over high heat.

2. When the water comes to a boil, drop in the diced zucchini to quickly parboil. Remove after about 10 seconds, drain well, and transfer to a large serving bowl. Cover to keep warm.

3. Drop the pasta into the boiling water and add a dash of olive oil. Cook the pasta according to package directions.

4. While the pasta is cooking, place the pine nuts in a heavy medium-sized skillet that has been preheated over medium-high heat. Heat, shaking the pan to keep the nuts moving, until the nuts turn golden in color. Remove the nuts from the pan and allow to cool.

5. Place a splash of olive oil in the skillet used for the pine nuts, and add the olives, tomatoes, rosemary, and garlic. Stir until well blended, and cook over medium heat just until hot. Add the parboiled zucchini at the last moment and stir to heat through.

6. Drain the pasta and divide among 4 to 6 prewarmed plates. Spoon the sauce evenly over each serving, sprinkle with the pine nuts and other garnishes, and serve immediately.

YIELD: 4–6 SERVINGS

I pound linguine, fettuccine, or other long flat pasta

1½ cups shredded cabbage

I tablespoon olive oil

6 ounces cottage cheese

½ teaspoon cracked black pepper

Salt to taste

I tablespoon sweet Hungarian paprika

HUNGARIAN NOODLES WITH CABBAGE AND COTTAGE CHEESE

While the combination of cabbage and cottage cheese may sound strange, this old-fashioned "comfort food" is wonderful— very smooth and mellow.

1. Fill a large pot with water, and bring to a boil over high heat. Drop in the pasta, and cook according to package directions.

2. Combine the cabbage and olive oil in a large skillet, and cook uncovered over medium heat for about 10 minutes, or until the cabbage is soft and just beginning to brown. Add the cottage cheese, pepper, and salt to taste, and stir to mix.

3. Drain the pasta and transfer to a prewarmed serving bowl. Add the cabbage mixture, and toss gently to combine. Sprinkle generously with paprika and serve immediately.

LAMB AND OLIVE STEW

*Lamb is much loved in the Mideast. When combined with olives
in this savory stew, it makes a delightful combination
that just may become a favorite at your house.*

1. Place the oil in a large skillet over medium heat. When the oil is hot, add the onions and cook, stirring occasionally, for about 7 minutes, or until translucent but not brown.

2. Add the lamb, green pepper, and garlic to the pot. Sprinkle with the cayenne and salt to taste. Cook, stirring often, for 5 to 7 minutes, or until the meat is browned on all sides.

3. While the lamb is cooking, place the water in a large saucepan and bring to a boil over high heat. Transfer the stew to the boiling water, using some of the water to deglaze the skillet if necessary. Reduce the heat, cover the pot, and simmer, stirring occasionally, for 1 hour, or until the meat is tender.

4. Stir the rice and olives into the stew. Cover and cook over low heat for another 20 minutes, or until most of the liquid has been absorbed and the rice is tender.

5. Stir in the fresh parsley and serve immediately.

YIELD: 4–6 SERVINGS

¼ cup olive oil

2 onions, finely chopped

1 pound lamb, cubed

1 green bell pepper, finely chopped

2 cloves garlic, crushed

⅛ teaspoon cayenne pepper

Salt to taste

2 cups water

1 cup white rice

14 pitted black olives, halved

3 tablespoons finely chopped fresh parsley

YIELD: **4** SERVINGS

¹/₄ cup olive oil

6 cloves garlic, finely minced

3 pounds ripe but firm plum tomatoes, cut into bite-sized chunks

1 pound unpeeled zucchini, cut into bite-sized chunks

2 large unpeeled eggplants, cut into bite-sized chunks

2 large onions, coarsely chopped

1 cup red wine

1 cup chopped fresh basil, or ¹/₄ cup dried basil

Salt and cracked pepper to taste

Red pepper flakes to taste

RATATOUILLE

This elegant French delight is undeniably one of my all-time favorite dishes. Whenever I visit family in Scottsdale, Arizona, I always fit in a visit to a small "boutique" restaurant that features authentic ratatouille. This recipe comes close.

1. Place the oil in a heavy stockpot over medium heat. When the oil is hot, add the garlic and cook, stirring occasionally, until soft but not brown.

2. Add the vegetables to the stockpot, and toss to coat with the oil. Stir in the wine and seasonings and cook uncovered, stirring occasionally, for about 30 minutes, or until the vegetables are tender and the liquid has evaporated. The vegetables should retain their shape, so don't let them get mushy.

3. Serve hot with chunks of French bread, use as a side dish, or serve chilled as a salad.

MEDITERRANEAN MEATLOAF

YIELD: ONE 5-X-9-INCH LOAF

This Greek-inspired meatloaf is made with ground turkey and lots of other good things, including a studding of Kalamata olives. Lighter in flavor than beef, turkey allows the flavors of the other ingredients to shine through. If you're lucky enough to have leftovers, be sure to make meatloaf sandwiches the next day.

I pound ground turkey

³/₄ cup unflavored bread crumbs or quick-cooking rolled oats

¹/₄ cup tomato sauce

¹/₄ cup tomato paste

2 eggs, beaten

¹/₃ cup chopped Kalamata olives

¹/₄ cup finely chopped onion

I small clove garlic, finely minced (optional)

¹/₄ cup finely chopped spinach

¹/₂ teaspoon salt

¹/₈ cup chopped parsley

¹/₄ teaspoon ground nutmeg

I ¹/₂ teaspoons fresh lemon juice

1. Place the turkey in a large bowl, and break it up a bit with your hands or a fork. Add the remaining ingredients in the order given, combining as you go along. Mix well.

2. Coat a 5-x-9-inch loaf pan with olive oil cooking spray, and place the turkey mixture in the pan. Bake in a preheated 350°F oven for 50 to 60 minutes, or until the loaf is firm and has begun to shrink from the sides of the pan.

3. Place the loaf pan on a wire rack and allow to rest for 10 minutes so that the loaf can absorb the juices. Slide a knife around the edges of the loaf, put a plate on top, and invert the pan so that the loaf slides onto the plate. Cut into thick slices and serve immediately.

Variation

For a striking variation of Mediterranean Meatloaf, omit the olives from the meatloaf mixture and divide the mixture in half. Place half of the loaf mixture in the bottom of the loaf pan, and arrange a row of stuffed olives down the center lengthwise, pushing the olives down to keep them in place. Place the remaining loaf mixture on top and press it down. Then bake the loaf according to the above directions. When you slice the meatloaf, you'll find a luscious olive in the center of each slice.

BREADS, MUFFINS, AND CAKES

OLD-FASHIONED OLIVE BREAD

YIELD: TWO 9-x-5-INCH LOAVES

1 1/4 cups boiling water

1/4 cup olive oil

2 tablespoons sugar

2 teaspoons salt

1 cup warm water

1 packet dry yeast

3 cups whole wheat flour

3 cups bread flour

1 1/2 cups rye flour

1/2 cup quartered green olives

1/2 cup quartered black olives

Olive oil

My family is very fond of good bread. I know every place for miles around that sells superlative "homemade" bread. However, I promise you, this olive bread—rich, mellow, and studded with both green and black olives—is better than anything you can buy anywhere.

1. Place the boiling water, olive oil, sugar, and salt in a large bowl, and stir until the sugar dissolves. Set aside and allow to cool for 20 to 30 minutes, or until the mixture is lukewarm.

2. Place the warm water in a small dish and sprinkle with the yeast. When the mixture bubbles, stir it into the lukewarm olive oil mixture.

3. Place the flours and olives in a large bowl, and stir to mix well. Stir the olive oil mixture into the flour.

4. Turn the dough onto a lightly floured board and knead for about 10 minutes, or until smooth and elastic.

5. Place the dough in a greased bowl, turn to grease all sides, and cover with a clean kitchen towel or plastic wrap. Allow the dough to rise in a warm place for about 45 minutes, or until doubled in bulk.

6. Punch the dough down and divide it into two parts. Shape each part to fit a 9-x-5-inch loaf pan, and place in a liberally oiled pan. Cover the loaves and allow to rise for 45 minutes, or until doubled in bulk.

7. Place the loaves in a preheated 400°F oven and bake for 40 to 50 minutes, or until the loaves sound hollow when you remove them from the pan and tap them on the bottom. Remove the loaves from the pans promptly, and brush the tops with olive oil. Place on a wire rack and allow to cool completely.

Variation

To make three different olive loaves, follow the instructions for Old-Fashioned Olive Bread through Step 4. Then continue with the following steps:

1. Divide the dough into two parts. Shape one part to fit a 9-x-5-inch loaf pan, and place in a liberally oiled pan.

2. Divide the remaining dough into two parts. Have ready ½ cup of Easy Olive Tapenade (page 120). Pat one part of the dough into an 8-x-6-inch rectangle, and spread three-fourths of the tapenade onto the dough, leaving a 1-inch border on each side. Roll the dough into a loaf, and place it seam-side down in a liberally oiled 9-x-5-inch loaf pan.

3. Form the remaining portion of dough into an 8-inch circle. Using your thumb, make several depressions in the top of the dough and spoon about ½ teaspoon of the remaining tapenade into each of the depressions. Transfer the mound to a liberally oiled metal pie plate.

4. Cover each of your creations with a clean kitchen towel or plastic wrap, and allow to rise in a warm place for about 45 minutes, or until doubled in bulk.

5. Place the loaves in a preheated 400°F oven and bake for 40 to 50 minutes, or until the loaves sounds hollow when you remove them from the pan and tap them on the bottom. Remove the loaves from the pans promptly, and brush the tops with olive oil. Place on a wire rack and allow to cool completely.

EASY OLIVE-RYE BREAD-MACHINE BREAD

YIELD: ONE 1-POUND LOAF

1¼ cups water

¼ cup olive oil

2½ cups rye flour

1 cup bread flour

¼ cup gluten

2 tablespoons sugar

1¼ teaspoons salt

¼ cup quartered green olives

¼ cup quartered black olives

1 packet dry yeast

This recipe makes what I call "Half a Loaf and Better Than Most."
Because it's a dense bread, it won't fully fill the bread chamber.
If you like a hearty loaf, please try it. It's very very good.

1. Place the water in the bread chamber and add the olive oil.

2. In a large bowl, combine the flours, sugar, and salt. Transfer about half of the mixture to the bread chamber, placing it on top of the liquid ingredients.

3. Dust the quartered olives with a little bit of the flour mixture and add them to the machine. Place the remainder of the dry ingredients in the bread chamber on top of the olives, and sprinkle the packet of yeast over all.

4. Place the baking chamber in the bread machine and set the controls to "whole wheat." When finished, remove the bread from the baking chamber promptly and cool on a wire rack.

Baking With Olive Oil

Baked goods made with olive oil are a real delight—moist and delicious. This chapter presents recipes for several baked treats, and from Old-Fashioned Olive Bread to Easy Devil's Food Cake, each is made with olive oil. But what if you want to replace the fat in your own recipes with the heart-healthy oil of the olive? If your recipe already uses oil, simply replace the usual product with the same quantity of olive oil. (See the inset on page 126 for guidance in choosing the best olive oil for your recipe.) If, on the other hand, your recipe uses butter, margarine, or another solid shortening, you should know that this product can't be replaced by olive oil on a cup-for-cup basis. Instead, use the following handy conversion chart, and enjoy the benefits of olive oil every time you bake.

OLIVE OIL SUBSTITUTION CHART

Amount of Butter, Margarine, or Other Solid Shortening		Equivalent Amount of Olive Oil
1 teaspoon	=	$3/4$ teaspoon
1 tablespoon	=	$2 1/4$ teaspoons
2 tablespoons	=	$1 1/2$ tablespoons
$1/4$ cup	=	3 tablespoons
$1/3$ cup	=	$1/4$ cup
$1/2$ cup	=	$1/4$ cup plus 2 tablespoons
$2/3$ cup	=	$1/2$ cup

YIELD: ABOUT 12 MUFFINS

2 cups bran cereal (not flakes), such as Kellogg's All-Bran cereal

1 1/4 cups milk, preferably nonfat

1 1/4 cups all-purpose flour

1 tablespoon baking powder

1/4 teaspoon salt

1/2 cup light or dark molasses

1/4 cup extra-light olive oil

2 eggs

2 tablespoons prune or apple purée baby food

1/2–3/4 cup dark or golden raisins

GRANDMA'S RAISIN-BRAN MUFFINS

My sister calls these "walk-around" bran muffins because they are so neat to eat. They are moist and don't shed crumbs, explaining why she begs me to make these for her when her office is having a breakfast meeting and everyone must bring something. While these yummy treats are perfect for toting just about anywhere, don't save them for a special occasion. Enjoy often.

1. Place the cereal and milk in a large bowl, and stir to combine. Set aside for about 5 minutes to soften.

2. Place the flour, baking powder, and salt in a medium-sized bowl, and stir to combine. Set aside.

3. When the bran is soft and has absorbed most of the milk, add the molasses, olive oil, eggs, and fruit purée. Stir until thoroughly combined.

4. Add about half of the flour mixture to the bran mixture, and stir with a large spoon to combine lightly.

5. Sprinkle the raisins on top of the batter. Sprinkle the rest of the flour mixture over the raisins, and stir just until combined. Do not overmix.

6. Grease 12 muffin cups or line with paper cups. Divide the batter equally among the 12 cups and bake in a preheated 400°F oven for 15 to 18 minutes, or until a toothpick inserted in the center of a muffin comes out clean. Allow to cool to room temperature before serving.

BANANA-NUT BREAD

YIELD: ONE 4-x-8-
INCH LOAF

Olive oil makes this bread both healthful and wonderfully moist.
This is a dense, fine-grained loaf that is even better the second day.
Remember, the more ripe and black the bananas, the better the flavor.

1. Place the bananas in a large mixing bowl, and mash with a fork or beat with an electric mixer. Add the white and brown sugars, and stir or beat to blend thoroughly. Drop in the eggs, and stir or beat to combine. Add the flours, baking soda, and salt, and combine. Add the oil to the batter a little at a time, mixing thoroughly. Finally, add the walnuts, and beat or stir to combine.

2. Generously grease a 4-x-8-inch loaf pan and turn the batter into the pan. Bake in a preheated 325°F oven for 50 to 60 minutes, or until a toothpick inserted in the center of the loaf comes out clean.

3. Allow the bread to cool in the pan for 10 minutes. Then turn the loaf onto a wire rack and cool completely before serving. This bread is even better the second day.

2 very ripe bananas

1/2 cup white sugar

1/2 cup brown sugar, packed

2 eggs

3/4 cup all-purpose flour

1/2 cup whole wheat flour

1 teaspoon baking soda

1/4 teaspoon salt

3/4 cup light olive oil

1/2 cup chopped walnuts

YIELD: ABOUT
24 COOKIES

3 very ripe bananas

$^{1}/_{3}$ cup light olive oil

1 egg

1 teaspoon vanilla
extract

$^{1}/_{8}$ teaspoon salt

1 $^{1}/_{2}$ cups quick-
cooking rolled oats

$^{1}/_{2}$ cup oat bran
cereal

1 $^{1}/_{2}$ cups coarsely
chopped dried fruit

$^{1}/_{2}$ cup coarsely
chopped walnuts

SUGARLESS AND FLOURLESS FRUIT AND NUT COOKIES

*These delectable morsels owe their sweetness to the dried fruits that stud
each cookie. Feel free to use any combination of dried fruits you like,
including the prechopped mixes now available in grocery stores.
If you want to chop your own fruit, use kitchen scissors,
which make the job fast and easy.*

1. Place the bananas in a large mixing bowl, and mash well with a fork.

2. Place the olive oil, egg, vanilla extract, and salt in a measuring cup, and whip with a fork to mix. Stir the olive oil mixture into the mashed bananas.

3. Stir the rolled oats and oat bran into the banana mixture, mixing well. Add the dried fruit and walnuts, and combine thoroughly.

4. Coat a large cookie sheet with olive oil cooking spray, and drop generously rounded tablespoons of the dough onto the sheet, spacing the cookies about 1$^{1}/_{2}$ inches apart to allow for spreading. Flatten each cookie gently with the back of a spoon.

5. Bake the cookies in a preheated 350°F oven for 18 to 20 minutes, or until the edges and bottoms of the cookies are lightly browned. Do not overbake.

6. Transfer the cookies to a wire rack or sheet of aluminum foil, and allow to cool completely before serving. These cookies crumble when hot.

HAPPY HEALTHY BROWNIES

YIELD: **12** BROWNIES

These intensely chocolatey brownies will make you happy for two reasons. First, they are very easy to prepare. Second, they are heart-healthy because olive oil takes the place of butter or other fats. And did I mention that they're moist, chewy, and utterly delicious?

1. Place the sugar, flour, cocoa powder, and salt in a large bowl, and stir to combine. Be sure that the cocoa is blended in well.

2. Place the eggs, olive oil, fruit purée, and vanilla extract in a small bowl, and beat with an electric mixer until well combined.

3. Add the wet ingredients to the dry ingredients and combine thoroughly with an electric mixer or a spoon. The batter will be stiff.

4. Grease a 9-x-13-inch baking pan, and push the batter into the pan. Resist the temptation to use a smaller pan. These brownies bake best when the batter is less than 1 inch deep.

5. Bake in a preheated 350°F oven for about 20 minutes, or until a toothpick inserted in the center comes out clean. Place the pan on a wire rack, and allow to cool for 10 minutes. Cut into squares while warm.

2 cups sugar

1 cup flour

$3/4$ cup cocoa powder

$1/4$ teaspoon salt

3 eggs

$1/2$ cup extra-light olive oil

2 tablespoons prune or apple purée baby food

1 teaspoon vanilla extract

YIELD: ONE 9-X-13-
INCH FLAT CAKE, OR
ONE BUNDT CAKE

1 box (1 pound,
2.25 ounces) devil's
food cake mix

1 package (4 ounces)
instant chocolate
pudding mix

3/4 cup extra-light
olive oil

5 eggs

1 teaspoon
vanilla extract

1 pound sour cream

EASY DEVIL'S FOOD CAKE

*This is another favorite at our house. This cake starts with a cake mix
and instant chocolate pudding. Yes, I know. It's been done before.
But this one is also enriched with sour cream and bakes up moist
and delicious. Enjoy it as is, dusted with powdered sugar,
or topped with your favorite frosting or glaze.*

1. Place the cake mix and instant pudding mix in a large bowl and mix lightly. Add the olive oil, eggs, and vanilla extract, and beat with an electric mixer until combined.

2. Add the sour cream to the cake batter, and beat with an electric mixer until thoroughly combined.

3. Grease a 9-x-13-inch baking pan or a 12-cup bundt pan. Pour the batter into the pan and bake in a preheated 350°F oven for 40 to 45 minutes for a sheet cake, or 50 to 55 minutes for a bundt cake. When the cake is done, a toothpick will come out clean when inserted in the center of the cake.

4. Cool the sheet cake completely before slicing and serving from the pan. Allow the bundt cake to rest for 10 minutes before inverting it onto a rack; then cool completely before slicing and serving.

Conclusion

Earlier in this book, you learned how ancient cultures believed the olive tree to be a gift of the gods. Certainly, no plant has proven to be more practical, enjoyable, and inspirational. We savor its fruit as a delicacy. We pour its glistening oil over salads, toss it into pastas, and drizzle it over breads. We use its leaves to relieve illness. We have adopted it as a symbol of peace and life. And we depict its magnificent form in works of art. Most of us can't get enough of the olive.

The Sophisticated Olive has been a sheer joy from beginning to end. I can't tell you how much I have loved researching, writing, and munching my way through this book. I hope that you have had as much fun reading your way through it, and that these pages have provided you with a greater appreciation of the olive. I also hope that I have inspired you to try many of the wonderful olives and olive oils of the world, as well as some of the scrumptious dishes (and drinks!) that can be made with the fruit of the olive tree.

The olive has long been a passion with me. Now that you've become better acquainted with the sophisticated olive, I hope that it becomes your passion, too.

METRIC CONVERSION TABLES

COMMON LIQUID CONVERSIONS

Measurement	=	Milliliters
$1/4$ teaspoon	=	1.25 milliliters
$1/2$ teaspoon	=	2.50 milliliters
$3/4$ teaspoon	=	3.75 milliliters
1 teaspoon	=	5.00 milliliters
$1 1/4$ teaspoons	=	6.25 milliliters
$1 1/2$ teaspoons	=	7.50 milliliters
$1 3/4$ teaspoons	=	8.75 milliliters
2 teaspoons	=	10.0 milliliters
1 tablespoon	=	15.0 milliliters
2 tablespoons	=	30.0 milliliters

Measurement	=	Liters
$1/4$ cup	=	0.06 liters
$1/2$ cup	=	0.12 liters
$3/4$ cup	=	0.18 liters
1 cup	=	0.24 liters
$1 1/4$ cups	=	0.30 liters
$1 1/2$ cups	=	0.36 liters
2 cups	=	0.48 liters
$2 1/2$ cups	=	0.60 liters
3 cups	=	0.72 liters
$3 1/2$ cups	=	0.84 liters
4 cups	=	0.96 liters
$4 1/2$ cups	=	1.08 liters
5 cups	=	1.20 liters
$5 1/2$ cups	=	1.32 liters

CONVERTING FAHRENHEIT TO CELSIUS

Fahrenheit	=	Celsius
200–205	=	95
220–225	=	105
245–250	=	120
275	=	135
300–305	=	150
325–330	=	165
345–350	=	175
370–375	=	190
400–405	=	205
425–430	=	220
445–450	=	230
470–475	=	245
500	=	260

CONVERSION FORMULAS

LIQUID		
When You Know	Multiply By	To Determine
teaspoons	5.0	milliliters
tablespoons	15.0	milliliters
fluid ounces	30.0	milliliters
cups	0.24	liters
pints	0.47	liters
quarts	0.95	liters

WEIGHT		
When You Know	Multiply By	To Determine
ounces	28.0	grams
pounds	0.45	kilograms

ResourceList

Throughout this book, you've learned about all the many delicious olives and olive oils produced throughout the world. Maybe you now can't wait to sample real Niçoise olives—but you just can't find them in your local stores. Or perhaps you're looking for an olive tree that you can grow and enjoy in your own backyard. Whatever your needs, this list will help by guiding you to companies that offer a selection of olive products, nurseries that carry olive trees, websites that provide information on olive cultivation, and much, much more. And whether you're looking for olive oil or olive plants, most of these companies will deliver your purchase right to your door.

Earthy Delights
1161 E. Clark Road, Suite 260
DeWitt, MI 48820
Phone: 800-367-4709
Website: www.earthy.com
A dizzying collection of fine olives, including Amfissa, Atalanti, Ionian, Kalamata, garlic-stuffed, apricot-stuffed, and sundried tomato-stuffed.

Norm Thompson
PO Box 3999
Portland, OR 97208
Phone: 800-547-1160
Website: www.normthompson.com
A range of olive products, including "tipsy olives," which have been marinated in fine French vermouth and stuffed with pimento paste; infused olive oils; and other treats for the olive lover.

The Olive Oil Source

390 Vista Grande
Greenbrae, CA 94904
Phone: 415-461-6267
Website: www.oliveoilsource.com

An incredible resource for olive lovers searching for superior olive oil; companies that sell olive trees, olive presses, and the like; companies that press your home-grown olives into oil; information on olive cultivation; and more.

Olive Pit

2156 Solano Street
Corning, CA 96021
Phone: 800-654-8374
Website: www.olivepit.com

A wonderful collection of olive products, from olive oils to Napa Valley Wine Olives, Texas Hot Chili Olives, Martini-Style Olives, and Mild Mustard Pitted Olives.

Pleasure Point Landscape

PO Box 364
Bangor, CA 95914
Phone: 530-679-2591
Website: www.olivetreemover.com

A selection of mature field-grown olive trees, including Sevillano, Mission, Manzanillo, and Kalamata.

Santa Barbara Olive Co.

12477 Calle Real
Santa Barbara, CA 93117
Phone: 800-624-4896
Website: www.sbolive.com

A wide variety of olives, infused olive oils, martini gift sets, dirty martini packs, and even herbal supplements with olive leaf extract.

Santa Cruz Olive Tree Nursery

Phone: 831-728-4269
Website: www.santacruzolive.com

A wide selection of one- and two-year-old olive varietals, including Frantoio, Leccino, Maurino, Pendolino, Coratina, Picholine, and Taggiasca.

Sur La Table

1765 Sixth Avenue South
Seattle, WA 98134-1608
Phone: 800-243-0852
Website: www.surlatable.com

Wonderful olive products and accessories, such as a delightful Provençal glazed terra cotta jar that holds two pounds of olives in brine, and a French porcelain olive oil jug.

3E Market

6753 Jones Mill Court, Suite A
Norcross, GA 30092-4379
Phone: 800-333-5548
Website: www.3emarket.com

A huge selection of special olives—including Alfonso, Gaeta, Kalamata, Niçoise, Picholines, Provençal, and more—as well as plain and flavored olive oils, and other gourmet products.

Williams-Sonoma

PO Box 379900
Las Vegas, NV 89137
Phone: 800-541-2233
Website: www.williams-sonoma.com

Everything for the olive-loving cook, including a wide selection of olive oils and olive oil dispensers.

Index

A

All-American Hot Potato Salad, 156

Almond (tasting term), 45

Al-Zitouna (The Olive Tree), 15

Antipasto Sandwich, The, 128

Appetizers. *See* Cocktails and party fare.

Arabian Olive, Onion, and Orange Salad, 152

Archives of Internal Medicine, The, 58

Athena, 8

Athenaeus, 11

Athens, 8

B

Baby Lima Beans With Garlic and Tarragon, 166

Banana-Nut Bread, 179

Basic Bruschetta, 118

Beauty and olive oil, 65–73

Beauty products, olive oil

Egg and Olive Oil Hair Conditioner, 73

Olive and Oats Moisturizing Lotion, 66

Olive Oil and Apple Toning Mask, 70–71

Olive Oil and Cream Face Cleanser, 67

Olive Oil and Egg Deep-Cleansing Mask, 70

Olive Oil and Egg Tightening Mask, 72

Olive Oil and Honey Hair Conditioner, 72

Olive Oil and Honey Softening Mask, 71

Olive Oil and Lemon Cream Face Cleanser, 69

Olive Oil and Strawberry Face Cleanser, 68

Olive Oil and Tea Eye
    Soother, 73
Beverages. *See* Martinis.
Bible, 13–14
Bitterness (tasting term), 45
Black Olives, 103–105
Botulism, 109
Breads, muffins, and cakes
    Banana-Nut Bread, 179
    Easy Devil's Food Cake, 182
    Easy Olive-Rye Bread-
        Machine Bread, 176
    Grandma's Raisin-Bran
        Muffins, 178
    Happy Healthy Brownies, 181
    Old-Fashioned Olive Bread,
        174–175
    Sugarless and Flourless Fruit
        and Nut Cookies, 180
Brigham and Women's
    Hospital, 59–60
Brine-Cured Olives, 108–109
British Medical Journal, 59
Brownies, Happy Healthy, 181
Bruschetta. *See* Cocktails and
    party fare.

C

Cakes. *See* Breads, muffins, and
    cakes.
Calmont, Jeanne, 65

Cancer and the olive, 57–59
Cardiovascular disease and the
    olive, 56–57, 61–62
Cato the Elder, 12
Cezanne, Paul, 21
Chanukah, 9
Cheese Bite Surprise, 117
Chinese Rice Salad, 154
Chunky Hot Pepper Dip, 123
Classic Cole Slaw, 142
Classic French Dressing, 138
Classic Italian Bread Salad, 155
Classic Vinaigrette, 135
Cleansers, facial. *See* Beauty
    products, olive oil.
Climate, 76–77, 80–81
Clovis I, 16–17
Cocktails and party fare
    Basic Bruschetta, 118
    Cheese Bite Surprise, 117
    Chunky Hot Pepper Dip, 123
    Dirty Martini, The, 113
    Easy Bruschetta, 120
    Easy Olive Tapenade, 120
    Eight-Layer Mexican Dip, 124
    Jessica's Special Stuffed
        Olives, 115
    Old-Style French Tapenade,
        122
    Olive and Garbanzo Bean
        Tapenade, 122

Olive Oil Refrigerator
    Pickles, 121
Perfect Dry Martini, The, 113
Spicy Marinated Olives, 116
Spinach Bruschetta With Feta
    Cheese, 119
Cold and Cough Compress, 63
Cole Slaw, Classic, 142
Cole Slaw, Greek, 143
Conditioners, hair. *See* Beauty
    products, olive oil.
Cookies, Sugarless and
    Flourless Fruit and Nut, 180
Cosmetics, olive oil. *See* Beauty
    products, olive oil.
Crete, 10
Curing olives, 25. *See also*
    Olives, homemade.

D

David, King, 14
Deipnosophistai, 11
Dioscorides, Pedanius, 11
Dips. *See* Cocktails and party
    fare.
Dirty Martini, The, 113
*Dispensatory of the United States
    of America, The*, 50–51
Dressings. *See* Salad dressings
    and sauces.
Dry Salt-Cured Olives, 106–107

E

Earthy (tasting term), 45
Easy Bruschetta, 120
Easy Devil's Food Cake, 182
Easy Olive Tapenade, 120
Easy Olive-Rye Bread-Machine
    Bread, 176
Ebla, 9
Eccentric chamber and rotor, 26
Egg and Olive Oil Hair
    Conditioner, 73
Eight-Layer Mexican Dip, 124
Eirene, 9
Elolenic acid, 60, 61
Entrées
    Hungarian Noodles With
        Cabbage and Cottage
        Cheese, 170
    Lamb and Olive Stew, 171
    Mediterranean Meatloaf, 173
    Mediterranean Vegetable
        Bake, 168
    Penne Pasta and Olives With
        Orange Zest, 169
    Ratatouille, 172
Extra virgin olive oil, 28

F

Fats
    hydrogenated, 54–55
    monounsaturated, 55
    polyunsaturated, 54
    saturated, 54
Fisherman's Soup, 160
Flavored olive oils, 30. *See also*
    Infused olive oils.
Fruitiness (tasting term), 45

G

Garden of Gethsemane, 14
Garlic-and-Rosemary-Infused
    Olive Oil, 133
Garlic-Infused Olive Oil, 130
Gazpacho, 161
Gladiators, 12
Grandma's Raisin-Bran Muffins,
    178
Greek Cole Slaw, 143
Greek Green Bean Salad, 153
Greek Vegetable Soup, 158
Greek-Inspired Garbanzo Picnic
    Salad, 146
Green Olives, 99–100
Grilled Shrimp Surprise Salad,
    151
Growing an olive tree, 22–23,
    76–86, 88–91

H

Hammer mill, 26
Happy Healthy Brownies, 181
Harmonious (tasting term), 45
Health, effects of olive tree on,
    50–65
Hearty Bean Soup, 159
Hearty Veggie Surprise
    Sandwich, 129
Hercules, 8–9
Hippocrates, 50
Homemade olives. *See* Olives,
    homemade.
Homer, 10
Hors d'oeuvres. *See* Cocktails
    and party fare.
Hot and Spicy Sicilian-Style
    Olives, 110
Hungarian Noodles With
    Cabbage and Cottage
    Cheese, 170

I

Infection and the olive, 60–61
Infused olive oils
    Garlic-and-Rosemary-
        Infused Olive Oil, 133
    Garlic-Infused Olive Oil, 130
    Lemon-Infused Olive Oil, 131
    Sundried Tomato and Thyme
        Olive Oil, 132
Isis, 8
Island Vegetable Salad, 149
Italian Antipasto Salad, 148
Italian Dressing, 137

Italian-Flag Dilled Vegetables, 157

J

Jefferson, Thomas, efforts of, to grow olive trees, 87
Jessica's Special Stuffed Olives, 115
Jesus, 14

K

Keys, Ancel, 56
Koran, 15

L

Lamb and Olive Stew, 171
Lampante, 29
Lemon-Infused Olive Oil, 131
Light Olive Oil, 30
Lye, using, 96–97

M

Martinis
    Dirty, The, 113
    history of, 114–115
    Perfect Dry, the, 113
Masks, facial. *See* Beauty products, olive oil.
Materia Medica, 50
Matisse, Henri, 21
Mayonnaise Mustard Sauce, 137

Medfly, 23
Mediterranean Meatloaf, 173
Mediterranean Vegetable Bake, 168
Metal toothed grinder, 26
Mission San Diego de Alcalá, 18
Mixer Mayo, 140
Mohammed, 15
Moisturizers. *See* Beauty products, olive oil.
Monte Testaccio, 16
Monticello, growing olives at, 87
Mount of Olives, 14
Muffins. *See* Breads, muffins, and cakes.
Musty (tasting term), 45

N

Natural History, 13
Natural remedies
    Cold and Cough Compress, 63
    Olive Leaf Tea, 62
    Olive Oil and St. John's Wort Liniment, 64
    Sinus Mask, 63
Nutritional value of the olive, 53, 56–62

O

Old-Fashioned Olive Bread, 174–175

Old-Style French Tapenade, 122
Olea Europaea. See Olive tree.
Oleuropein, 25, 52–53, 60, 61, 62
Olive and Garbanzo Bean Tapenade, 122
Olive and Garbanzo Salad, 145
Olive and Oats Moisturizing Lotion, 66
Olive Butter, 139
Olive fruit fly, 23
Olive leaf
    and caesars, 9, 12
    and cardiovascular health, 61–62, 65
    fossilized remains of, 10
    and infection, 60–61
Olive Leaf Tea, 62
Olive oil
    baking with, 177
    and beauty, 65–74
    and cancer, 57–59
    and cardiovascular health, 56–57
    choosing, for recipes, 126
    grades of, 27–30, 126
    infused. *See* Infused olive oils.
    and osteoporosis, 59
    producing, 26–27
    storing, 46–47
    and strength and youth, 9, 11
    tastings, guidelines for, 44–45

and weight loss, 59–60

Olive Oil and Apple Toning Mask, 70–71

Olive Oil and Cream Face Cleanser, 67

Olive Oil and Egg Deep-Cleaning Mask, 70

Olive Oil and Egg Tightening Mask, 72

Olive Oil and Honey Hair Conditioner, 72

Olive Oil and Honey Softening Mask, 71

Olive Oil and Lemon Cream Face Cleanser, 69

Olive Oil and St. John's Wort Liniment, 64

Olive Oil and Strawberry Face Cleanser, 68

Olive Oil and Tea Eye Soother, 73

Olive Oil Refrigerator Pickles, 121

Olive Oil-Roasted Potatoes, 165

Olive tree
   about, 20–22
   balled-and-burlapped plant, 81–82, 83
   bare-root plant, 82–83
   caring for an, 86, 88–91
   container-grown, 81–82, 83, 84

gift of, from Athena, 8

growing an, 22–23, 76–86, 88–91

in paintings, 21

as symbol of Olympic Games, 9, 11

Olives
   of Australia, 38–39
   of California, 40–41
   of Central and South America, 39–40
   curing, 25. *See also* Olives, homemade.
   of France, 37–38
   of Greece, 37
   harvesting, 23–24
   healing properties of, 50–51
   history of, 10–18
   of Italy, 36
   of the Middle East, 32–33
   of Morocco, 34–35
   nutritional value of, 52–53
   pressing, 26–27
   reverence for, 10
   of Spain, 35–36
   storing, 46–47
   as symbol of peace, 9, 13
   and traditions, 9
   of Tunisia, 34
   varieties of, 42–43

Olives, homemade
   Black Olives, 103–105
   Brine-Cured Olives, 108–109
   Dry Salt-Cured Olives, 106–107
   Green Olives, 99–100
   Hot and Spicy Sicilian-Style Olives, 110
   Spanish-Style Green Olives, 101–102
   Spicy Marinated Olives, 116

Olympic Games, 9, 11

Open-Faced Mushroom Sandwich, 127

Osteoporosis and the olive, 59

Oven-Roasted Dirty Potatoes, 166

P

Palmyra, 15

Pecan-Olive Cream Cheese Spread, 125

Penne Pasta and Olives With Orange Zest, 169

Perfect Dry Martini, The, 113

Pharmaceutical Journal of Provincial Transactions, 51

Philistines, 15

Phoenicia, 10

Pickles, Olive Oil Refrigerator, 121

Pindar, 9
Pliny the Elder, 13
Poseidon, 8
Pungency (tasting term), 45
Pure olive oil, 29

R

Rancid (tasting term), 45
Ratatouille, 172
Ready-When-You-Are Roasted
    Garlic, 162
Rémoulade Sauce, 141
Renoir, Pierre Auguste, 21
Richelieu, Julio, 114
Ripe Olive and Cream Cheese
    Spread, 125
Roasted Green Beans, 167
Roasted Mixed Vegetables, 163
Roasted Peppers in Marinade,
    164
Roasted Portabella Mushrooms,
    165
Rockefeller, John D., 114
Roosevelt, Franklin Delano,
    114–115
Rotor and screen grinder, 26
Rough (tasting term), 45

S

Salad dressings and sauces
    Classic French Dressing, 138

Classic Vinaigrette, 135
Italian Dressing, 137
Mayonnaise Mustard Sauce,
    137
Mixer Mayo, 140
Olive Butter, 139
Rémoulade Sauce, 141
Spicy Vinaigrette With
    Cilantro, 136
Sweet and Sassy Citrus
    Vinaigrette, 136
Tart and Spicy Vinaigrette,
    135
Thomas Jefferson's Favorite
    Dressing, 134
Tomato-Soup French
    Dressing, 139
Salade Niçoise, 144
Salads
    All-American Hot Potato
        Salad, 156
    Arabian Olive, Onion, and
        Orange Salad, 152
    Chinese Rice Salad, 154
    Classic Cole Slaw, 142
    Classic Italian Bread Salad,
        155
    Greek Cole Slaw, 143
    Greek Green Bean Salad, 153
    Greek-Inspired Garbanzo
        Picnic Salad, 146

Grilled Shrimp Surprise
    Salad, 151
Island Vegetable Salad, 149
Italian Antipasto Salad, 148
Italian-Flag Dilled
    Vegetables, 157
Olive and Garbanzo Salad,
    145
Salade Niçoise, 144
Strawberry and Red Onion
    Summer Salad, 150
Sunny Mediterranean Olive
    and Orange Salad, 152
Tabbouleh, 147
Sandwich spreads and
    sandwiches
    Antipasto Sandwich, 128
    Hearty Veggie Surprise
        Sandwich, 129
    Open-Faced Mushroom
        Sandwich, 127
    Pecan-Olive Cream Cheese
        Spread, 125
    Ripe Olive and Cream
        Cheese Spread, 125
    Stuffed Olives and Cream
        Cheese Spread, 130
Santorini, 10
Sauces. See Salad dressings and
    sauces.
Saul, King, 14

Sinai and Palestine in Connection With Their History, 14–15

Sinus Mask, 63

Soil, 77–78

Solon, 10

Soups
   Fisherman's Soup, 160
   Gazpacho, 161
   Greek Vegetable Soup, 158
   Hearty Bean Soup, 159

Spanish-Style Green Olives, 101–102

Spicy Marinated Olives, 116

Spicy Vinaigrette With Cilantro, 136

Spinach Bruschetta With Feta Cheese, 119

Stanley, Arthur Penrhyn, 14

Stone olive mill, 26

Strawberry and Red Onion Summer Salad, 150

Strigil, 11

Strong's Exhaustive Concordance, 13

Stuffed Olives and Cream Cheese Spread, 130

Sugarless and Flourless Fruit and Nut Cookies, 180

Sundried Tomato and Thyme Olive Oil, 132

Sunny Mediterranean Olive and Orange Salad, 152

Sweet and Sassy Citrus Vinaigrette, 136

T

Tabbouleh, 147

Tapenades. *See* Cocktails and party fare.

Tart and Spicy Vinaigrette, 135

Thomas Jefferson's Favorite Dressing, 134

Tomato-Soup French Dressing, 139

V

Van Gogh, Vincent, 21

Varieties of olives, 42–43

Vegetables
   Baby Lima Beans With Garlic and Tarragon, 166

Olive Oil-Roasted Potatoes, 165

Oven-Roasted Dirty Potatoes, 166

Ready-When-You-Are Roasted Garlic, 162

Roasted Green Beans, 167

Roasted Mixed Vegetables, 163

Roasted Peppers in Marinade, 164

Roasted Portabella Mushrooms, 165

Verticillium wilt, 23

Vinaigrettes. *See* Salad dressings and sauces.

Virgil, 49

Virgin olive oil, 28–29

W

Weight loss and the olive, 59–60

Winey (tasting term), 45

Z

Zeus, 8

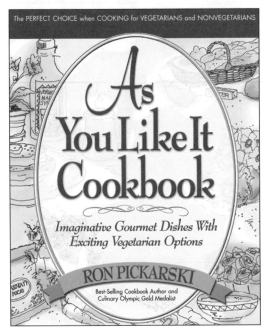

AS YOU LIKE IT COOKBOOK

Imaginative Gourmet Dishes with Exciting Vegetarian Options

Ron Pickarski

When it comes to food, we certainly like to have it our way. However, catering to individual tastes can pose quite a challenge for the cook. Have you ever prepared a wonderful dish, but because it contained beef or chicken, your daughter-in-law, the vegetarian, wouldn't go near it? To meet the challenge of cooking for vegetarians and nonvegetarians alike, celebrated chef Ron Pickarski has written the *As You Like It Cookbook*.

Designed to help you find the perfect meals for today's contemporary lifestyles, the *As You Like It Cookbook* offers over 175 great-tasting dishes that cater to a broad range of tastes. Many of the easy-to-follow recipes are already vegetarian—and offer ingredient alternatives for meat eaters. Conversely, recipes that include meat, poultry, or fish offer nonmeat ingredient options. Furthermore, if the recipe includes eggs or dairy products, a vegan alternative is given for those who follow a strictly plant-based diet. This book has it all—delicious breakfast favorites, satisfying soups and sandwiches, mouth-watering entrées and side dishes, and delectable desserts.

So don't despair the next time someone asks what's for dinner. With the *As You Like It Cookbook,* a tantalizing meal—cooked exactly as your family likes it—is just minutes away.

$16.95 • 216 pages • 7.5 x 9-inch quality paperback • 8 Full-Color Pages • ISBN 0-7570-0013-4

KITCHEN QUICKIES
Great, Satisfying Meals in Minutes
Marie Caratozzolo and Joanne Abrams

Have you ever left work after a long, hard day feeling totally exhausted, but knowing that the second you arrive home, you have to make a meal, *fast*? Or maybe you've spent the day driving your kids from soccer practice to play dates. Now everyone's clamoring for dinner. But is it possible to get a home-cooked meal on the table before, say, midnight? Absolutely!

The authors of *Kitchen Quickies* know that in this busy world, you just don't have time for hours of grocery shopping followed by hours of food preparation. Their solution? To begin with, virtually all of their over 170 kitchen-tested recipes

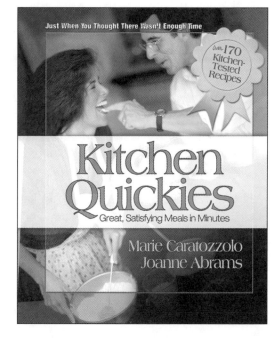

call for a maximum of five ingredients other than kitchen staples. This makes shopping easier. Then the dish itself takes at most forty-five minutes to prepare. And these delicious dishes are actually good for you—low in fat and high in nutrients!

Kitchen Quickies begins by guiding you through the basics of quick-and-easy cooking. Following this are ten spectacular chapters filled with exciting and imaginative dishes, including sensational soups, satisfying sandwiches, refreshing salads, fabulous pastas, tempting chicken and turkey dishes, sizzling seafood, hearty beef and pork fare, meatless delights, enticing vegetable and grain side dishes, and luscious desserts. In *Kitchen Quickies,* you'll learn how to make tangy Margarita Chicken, Savory Crab Cakes, saucy Penne from Heaven, and more—all in no time flat!

So the next time you think that there's simply no time to cook a good meal, pick up *Kitchen Quickies.* Who knows? You may even have time for a few quickies of your own.

$14.95 • 240 pages • 7.5 x 9-inch paperback • 16 Full-Color Pages • ISBN 0-7570-0085-1

CONFESSIONS OF A COFFEE BEAN

The Complete Guide to Coffee Cuisine

Marie Nadine Antol

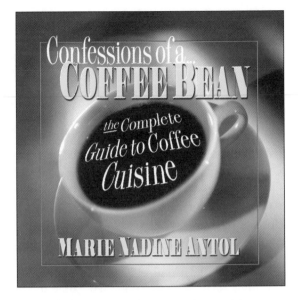

Yes, I have a few things to confess. But before I start, I just want you to know that I couldn't help it. It just happened. Everywhere I went, they wanted me. Now, I have a few things to share—I think it's time to spill the beans.

With a distinct aroma and an irresistible flavor, it has commanded the attention of the world. It is the coffee bean, and while many seek its pleasures, few know its secrets—the secrets of its origin and its appeal, and the key to getting the best out of the bean. Designed for lovers of coffee everywhere, here is a complete guide to understanding and enjoying this celebrated object of our affection.

Part One of Confessions of a Coffee Bean opens with the history of coffee and details the coffee bean's epic journey from crop to cup. It then describes the intriguing evolution of the coffeehouse, highlights surprising facts about coffee and your health, and provides an introduction to the most enticing coffees available today. Finally, this section presents everything you need to know about making a great cup of coffee, from selecting the beans to brewing a perfect pot.

Part Two is a tempting collection of recipes for both coffee drinks and coffee accompaniments. First, you'll learn to make a wide variety of coffee beverages, from steaming brews like Café au Lait to icy concoctions like the Espresso Shake. Then, you'll enjoy a bevy of desserts and other coffee companions, from classic crumb-topped cakes to coffee-kissed creations such as Rich Coffee Tiramisu. You'll even find recipes for coffee-laced candies and sauces.

Whether you're a true coffee aficionado or just someone who loves a good cup of java, this is a book that will entrance you with fascinating facts about all things coffee.

$13.95 • 204 pages • 7.5 x 7.5-inch quality paperback • 2-Color • 0-7570-0020-7

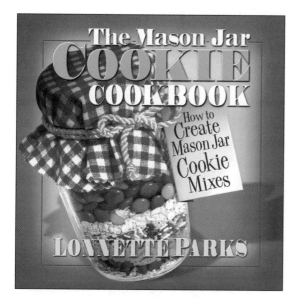

THE MASON JAR COOKIE COOKBOOK
How to Create Mason Jar Cookie Mixes

Lonnette Parks

Nothing gladdens the heart like the tantalizing aroma of cookies baking in the oven. But for so many people, a busy lifestyle has made it impossible to find the time to bake at home—until now. Lonnette Parks, cookie baker extraordinaire, has not only developed fifty kitchen-tested recipes for delicious cookies, but has found a way for you to give the gift of home baking to everyone on your gift list.

For each mouth-watering cookie, the author provides the full recipe so that you can bake a variety of delights at home. In addition, she provides complete instructions for beautifully arranging the nonperishable ingredients in a Mason jar so that you can give the jar—complete with baking instructions—to a friend. By adding just a few common ingredients, such as butter and eggs, your friend can then prepare fabulous home-baked cookies in a matter of minutes. Recipes include Best Ever Chocolate Chip Cookies, Blondies, Cranberry Dream Drops, Gingerbread Cookies, Oatmeal Raisin Cookies, and much, much more.

Whether you want to bake scrumptious cookies in your own kitchen, you'd like to give distinctive Mason jar cookie mixes to cookie-loving friends and family, or you're searching for a unique fund-raising idea, *The Mason Jar Cookie Cookbook* is the perfect book. It just may bring home-baked cookies back in style.

$12.95 • 144 pages • 7.5 x 7.5-inch paperback • 2-Color • ISBN 0-7570-0046-0

THE MASON JAR SOUP-TO-NUTS COOKBOOK
How to Create Mason Jar Recipe Mixes
Lonnette Parks

Walk into any gift or gourmet store, and you'll see that the popularity of beautiful Mason Jar mixes continues to grow. In this follow-up to her best-selling book, *The Mason Jar Cookie Cookbook,* author and cook extraordinaire Lonnette Parks presents recipes for more than fifty delicious soups, muffins, scones, breads, cakes, brownies, pancakes, beverages, and more—as well as some great treats for your pets. And, just as in her previous book, the author tells you how to give the gift of home cooking to friends and family.

For each Mason jar creation, the author provides the full recipe so that you can cook or bake a variety of delights at home. In addition, she includes complete instructions for beautifully arranging the nonperishable ingredients in a Mason jar so that you can give the jar—complete with preparation instructions—to a friend. By adding just a few common ingredients, your friend can then prepare mouthwatering baked goods, refreshing beverages, and satisfying soups and breakfast dishes in a matter of minutes. Recipes include Golden Corn Bread, Double Chocolate Biscotti, Ginger Muffins, Apple Cinnamon Pancakes, Barley Rice Soup, Viennese Coffee, and much, much more.

Whether you're interested in cooking a stack of golden pancakes in your own kitchen, giving distinctive Mason jar recipe mixes to friends and family, or searching for a clever fund-raising idea, *The Mason Jar Soup-to-Nuts Cookbook* is the perfect book.

$12.95 • 144 pages • 7.5 x 7.5-inch paperback • 2-Color • ISBN 0-7570-0129-7 • Available March 2003

For more information about our books,
visit our website at www.squareonepublishers.com